Contemporary Printmaking in Japan

Designed and produced in Japan by Zokeisha Publications Limited,
9 Azabu-Roppongi, Minato-ku, Tokyo, and published in the U.S.A. by
Crown Publishers, Inc., 419 Park Avenue South, New York.

Printed in Japan

Contemporary Printmaking in Japan

by Ronald G. Robertson

Crown Publishers, Inc.

NEW YORK

Contents

Preface

Much has been written about contemporary Japanese prints, but relatively little of this writing focuses on the process by which such prints are made. Indeed, the written word probably cannot adequately convey the art of the printmaker, for that art is best understood if it is experienced directly, or is at least seen. For this reason I have relied upon visual material wherever possible to demonstrate the techniques and prints of the six artists and to illustrate the chapter on the basic Japanese wood-block printing methods.

Choosing wood-block artists, to the exclusion of artists working in other media, attests to my conviction that the field of wood-block prints is one of the most fertile in contemporary Japanese art. I selected just six artists, from perhaps a hundred or more now active in Japan, in order to present fully the contrasts of method and expression employed—contrasts that are equally reflected in their opinions about their art. To present such material directly and simply, I have limited explanations and photographs of each artist's work to the techniques he used in the preparation and printing of a single print. I hope that an understanding of these techniques and of the attitudes behind them will stimulate the reader to experiment for himself, to expand upon the ideas offered here.

I wish to express thanks to my wife Helen, who has assisted in the research from the beginning; to Mr. Yuji Abé, Director of the Yoseido Gallery, who was instrumental in arranging the interviews with the artists; to Dr. and Mrs. Jack von Dornum and Dr. Ivan Benson for their invaluable help with the editing; to Miss Hideko Urushibara and Mr. Rei Yuki for their assistance in translation; to Miss Toyo Hayashi for typing the text; to Mr. Peter T. Fujita for processing the photographic materials; and to Mr. Shokichi Kobayashi for his demonstration of *baren* making. My greatest debt is to the six artists, who gave so generously of their time and art. To all I extend my sincere appreciation.

R. G. R.

A Brief Survey

"In Art, tradition is to create not revive....
If revival had been a continuing virtue, we
would still be painting hunting scenes on the
walls of caves...."

Since wood-block prints, one of modern Japan's most significant art forms, have again received widespread international recognition, one should no longer be astonished to see that they are so unlike the traditional prints known as *ukiyo-e*. It was more than a century ago that the elegant *ukiyo-e* of the *Edo* period first made their influence felt in a Europe that was ripe for new sources of inspiration. Many Western artists of the late nineteenth century were strongly influenced by the Japanese print with its emphasis on a frankly two-dimensional, non-naturalistic outline, its bold foreshortening, its extremely sensitive line and color and the unusual composition. The influence was by no means a one-way affair, for modern Western art—introduced into Japan by landmark exhibitions (Tokyo, 1913, 1914) of works by Van Gogh, followed by those of Monet, Pissarro and Bonnard—had a tremendous impact on Japanese artists. From that moment on, stimulated by works and reproductions of Western artists that became increasingly available, the Japanese were no longer content to be provincial artists. The European artists who had been so influenced by the Japanese print and their successors were to repay their debt a hundredfold in ideas that led to Japan's adoption of the full international style, with its characteristic abstract and expressionistic idiom.

The contemporary Japanese wood-block movement completes a circle that had its origin in China, traced a path through Europe and returned to stimulate a rebirth of what is now one of the most fertile art expressions in Japan. Wood-block printing was first introduced into Europe from the Orient by the caravan traders and Christian missionaries. Because it arrived in Europe before paper was available, the technique was initially used for printing fabrics. By the end of the fourteenth century, however, paper mills were in active production in Germany, France and Italy, and wood-block prints on paper made their appearance. It is significant to note here that the development of paper in China can be traced back to about the second century and relates to the early development of the wood-block print in the Orient. The first woodcuts made in Europe were religious mementos and playing cards that were frequently colored by hand in the same manner as the early Japanese woodcuts. Even now, the contemporary traditionalist, Shiko Munakata, frequently applies colors to the back of his prints by hand in a similar fashion. Early European wood-block artists, like the Japanese, used a process of relief carving until the time of Thomas Bewick in the eighteenth century, when wood engraving—a technique utilizing the end grain of the wood—was invented.

No other art form is so deeply rooted in Japan as the woodcut. One of the oldest Japanese woodcuts is dated in the eighth century. (Credit for the invention of the wood-block print belongs to China of a still earlier period.) Moreover, wood-block printing was the only means of pictorial reproduction known to the Japanese until trade with the West began. The first woodcuts, used to disseminate devotional pictures designed by Buddhist priests, were primitive black and white prints—still a source of inspiration to contemporary artists—that were made by pasting the design of the artist onto the plank of wood; that is, with the grain—not the end grain—and by removing the surface of the wood around and between the lines of the design. Printing ink was then applied to the parts of the block left in relief, paper laid on the block and rubbed from the back and an impression taken. The artist never cut the blocks himself but only furnished the design. By the fifteenth century, the block cutter had obtained a high degree of skill, and the woodcuts were used to embellish certain Buddhistic scrolls. But, again, only the outline was printed as a basis for painting in areas defined in the same manner as in a child's coloring book. After a period of recession, there was a sudden output of illustrated books from about 1650 onward, published to meet the immense demand of the public for books of legend, poetry, history, and fiction of every kind.

The first *ukiyo-e* prints appeared as illustrations for books and, a little later, in album form. The term *ukiyo-e* itself, means painting of the "floating world," a name used to describe the art dealing with the pleasures of the common people. At first, especially in the seventeenth century, it was a school of painting, but later it became synonymous with the wood-block prints of that period, and as such it is chiefly known today. Hishikawa Moronobu, an early *Edo* artist, chiefly responsible for the change from painting to wood-block prints, created an art that could be produced in large enough quantities to satisfy a public demand. The earliest *ukiyo-e* prints were made in black and white, but color was soon added, first by hand and later by the use of additional blocks that added red and green. The fully developed color print, called *nishiki-e* or brocade picture, was the creation of the eighteenth-century artist, Suzuki Harunobu, considered the father of the Japanese color print. He, along with Kiyonaga, Utamaro, Sharaku, Hokusai and Hiroshige, was one of the great masters of the *ukiyo-e* print.

It is a tribute to the greatness of these masters that the *ukiyo-e* print, considering its method of production and its purpose, developed into a significant art form. For the *ukiyo-e* prints were created in circumstances of extraordinary difficulty. These prints were the product of a group effort—the artist who composed the block design, the engraver who carved the wood block, and the printer who made the final copy. This group of three was subject to the whims of often dictatorial publishers, who could criticize and advise at any stage of the process.

And they were restricted by official censorship and restraints on the use of printing media. Finally, the *ukiyo-e* was intended to advertise *kabuki* and the pleasures of the *Yoshiwara* district and to entertain the rising middle class. These mundane purposes induced the Japanese to look upon the prints as ordinary commercial items that could never command a significant place in Japanese fine art. Even today wood-block prints bear this stigma, though to a lesser degree, in Japan. The insignificance of the *ukiyo-e* print as a fine art form is well attested by the manner in which, to the later regret of the Japanese collectors, the prints were casually used and randomly exported. Van Gogh, for example, discovered that a canister of Japanese green tea he had purchased was wrapped in one of these prints. Neglected at home, the *ukiyo-e* were given high praise in Europe and contributed to the development of Impressionism. But despite this international acceptance and acclaim, the *ukiyo-e* declined in Japan. With the death of Hiroshige in 1858, and in a post-Meiji Japan, the social conditions and the craftsmanship that had once made the *ukiyo-e* possible no longer existed. Only one modern artist, Goyo Hashiguchi (1880–1921), sought to revive *ukiyo-e* wood-block printing, and then only briefly. Moreover, his prints, even those of Japanese beauties, showed the Western influence. The prints of Hasue Kawase (1883–   ) and Hiroshi Yoshida (1876–1950, father of Hodaka Yoshida), helped to perpetuate the tradition of wood-block printing and perhaps expressed the taste of modern Japan more successfully than those of Goyo Hashiguchi. Their work contributed little, however, to the artistic revolution, imported from Europe, that was sweeping Japan or to the consequent development of *hanga*, the modern Japanese print movement.

The modern Japanese print is not a revival of the *nishiki-e,* as the polychrome wood-block printing method used by the *ukiyo-e* artists was called, but combines the best of the international style with the permanent components of a traditional Japanese method. It made a new start from an entirely different source, when several artists, notably Kanae Yamamoto (1882–1946) and Koshiro Onchi (1891–1955), sensitive to the movements of modern art in Europe, were attracted by modern European prints, and especially by the stark black and white woodcuts of the Norwegian, Edvard Munch. It was almost as if the Japanese artists had discovered the medium of wood block for the first time, for the *ukiyo-e* had long ceased to be a popular or significant expression in their own country and the later development of mechanical printing devices and consequent mass-production techniques had completed its decline. The *ukiyo-e* had achieved the highest possible peak of development without having its artistic value recognized in Japan, then had come to an end and degenerated into a mere handicraft for faithfully reproducing original drawings, older prints and paintings. It was during this latter, blank period, in which virtually everything from the past wood-block tradition was artistically extinct, that the modern Japanese print was reborn. Although these new prints were at first mere imitations of European prints, the Japanese artist, as he gained experience, began to introduce color and to borrow from his own tradition those techniques most suitable to the new expression. Some discovered the wood block to be a uniquely suitable medium for abstract design. Others, having struggled with Western techniques, returned eagerly to the Japanese way. Wood-block printing, moreover, was an expression with which they could more honestly identify themselves. For many, oil painting was European and a medium that had no roots in Japan. (One exception occurs, oddly, in a seventh-century painting—one of the oldest oil paintings in the world—on the *Tamamushi* shrine in the *Horyu-ji* at Nara. However, the technique using oil paint, called *mitsudo*, was not developed further after that period.) The pioneers of the modern Japanese print borrowed the techniques of the *ukiyo-e* artists, but they did not allow themselves to be limited by a method whose content and manufacture they deemed obsolete. To be free, they protested, the artist must carve his own blocks; choose his own colors; and print his own work. Thus, the *sosaku hanga,* translated as individual creative print, to distinguish it from the *ukiyo-e,* developed. For the first time in Japan the print was brought under the control of the artist.

Unquestionably, there is now a renaissance of printmaking, not only in Japan, but in the West as well. The print is becoming a potent rival of the painting, which it had, a short time ago, only supplemented. The past twenty five years have seen more technical innovations than have all the previous centuries. This development is evidenced by the many international print exhibitions and also by the fact that prints have received recognition and prizes as equals in mixed media exhibits. Fortunately, an increasing number of people who are becoming actively interested in art not only want to see works of art but also wish to own them. Since most paintings of significance are usually too imposing or large and costly for the home —and reproductions, even though good, are not entirely satisfactory—many are turning to creative prints as a solution to their need for original art on a scale they can comfortably live with. It is in no small measure owing to the creative productions of both the contemporary and the traditional Japanese wood-block artists that wood-block prints have attained such high favor in the international art milieu.

I. Basic Wood-Block Printing Methods

Laymen or beginners often feel that the print utilizing the greatest number of colors and techniques is a better print than one utilizing a single color and technique. In actuality, a single-color print that is well thought out and sensitively done has more value than an inept ten-color, multitechnical print. For the beginner especially, the composition of the print and the techniques used should be simple and direct.

Selection of the Wood

The first step is to choose the wood—one that has an even, close grain that can be cut cleanly with the tool (Ia). Cherry, pear, boxwood, willow, lauan, linden, silver magnolia and maple are some of the woods that have these qualities. Some hardwoods are too dense to be readily carved, while softer, unseasoned woods have a tendency to split and mar easily. Plywoods, used as well as the solid plank, have a surface layer that (with the exception of the marine types) can be easily "peeled," eliminating the need to carve out manually large areas of the block (119, page102). Moreover, plywood can be obtained in the large sizes needed for large prints.

Weathered woods or those found in old furniture often are well seasoned and have much character. The grained, relief textures, knotholes and nailheads found in such woods can be utilized in the print. Generally the surface of the wood should be smooth and level. If not, it may be necessary to plane or sand the surface. If the block is warped, it can be flattened by wetting and placing it under pressure.

Occasionally, an end-grain block (Ib) is used. However, this type of block is primarily for wood engraving which has its own specialized tools and technical requirements.

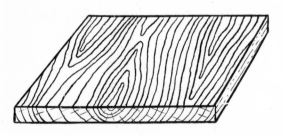

Ia. Plank of board

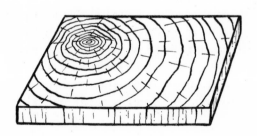

Ib. End grain

The Tools

A great variety of wood-block tools are available, but a few well chosen and of good quality suffice for most of the carving techniques necessary. A minimum set should include one or two of each of the following five basic tools illustrated (II).

The Japanese knife (IIa) is a precise, flexible tool that must be held and used correctly for good results. Grip the handle of the tool and incline both the tool and hand to the right so that the blade of the tool enters the wood at an approximate 60° angle (IV). Maintaining this angle, pull the tool firmly toward the body. This action makes the first of two cuts for carving a "line" (IVa). If the design or drawing on the block is curved or varied, do not change the position of the hand or tool, but move and reposition the block to change the direction of the cut. To complete the cutting of the "line," turn the block around, grip the tool in the correct manner and cut the second or opposing side of the "line" (IVb). If the second cut is made properly, a V-shaped shaving can be lifted

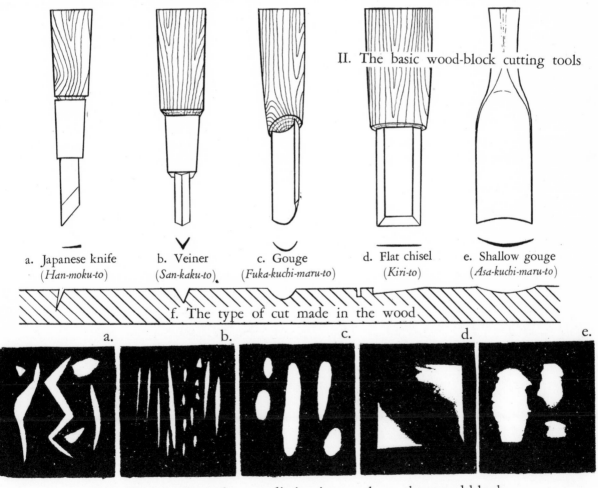

II. The basic wood-block cutting tools

a. Japanese knife (Han-moku-to)   b. Veiner (San-kaku-to)   c. Gouge (Fuka-kuchi-maru-to)   d. Flat chisel (Kiri-to)   e. Shallow gouge (Asa-kuchi-maru-to)

f. The type of cut made in the wood

a.   b.   c.   d.   e.

III. Each tool produces a distinctive mark on the wood-block

11

out of the double-cut "line" (IVc).

The veiner (IIb), gouge (IIc,e) and chisel (IId) are pushed away from the body. Hold this type of tool between the thumb and index fingers of the right hand. Place the left thumb on the tool (in front of the right thumb) to act as a guide during the carving (V). Before working with these tools, check the direction of the grain of the wood block. Push the tool along the grain (VI), because pushing against the grain tends to drag and tear the wood (VII).

To "outline" any forms that must stand in relief, use either the Japanese knife or the veiner. Then use the flat chisel (in this case, across the grain) to remove the surrounding negative areas. If the area to be removed is extensive, hold the chisel in the left hand, and tap the handle with the mallet. The tool moves from right to left across the wood grain. If the block is plywood, push the blade of the chisel under the surface layer of ply and "peel" it off. Use either the chisel or

shallow gouge to clean up any unwanted areas from the negative backgrounds.

If a cross section were made of the block, the areas in relief would have a wide base (VIIIa) and not an overhanging edge that was formed by undercutting the relief (VIIIb). The undercut areas are not only weak but also capture printing media and blur the print.

A bench hook (IX) can be easily made to hold the block in place for greater ease and safety in carving the blocks.

It is extremely important to keep the tools sharp. A dull tool requires more effort and does not cut cleanly. To sharpen the tools, use a whetstone or an oilstone. Place only the beveled edge of the blade, the gray areas in (Xa), on the surface of the stone and push the tool forward (Xb). Return the tool to the starting position without pressure and repeat the action until the tool is sharpened. Note: The gouge must be simultaneously rotated and pushed forward (Xb).

IV. Cutting with the Japanese knife

V. Cutting with the veiner

12

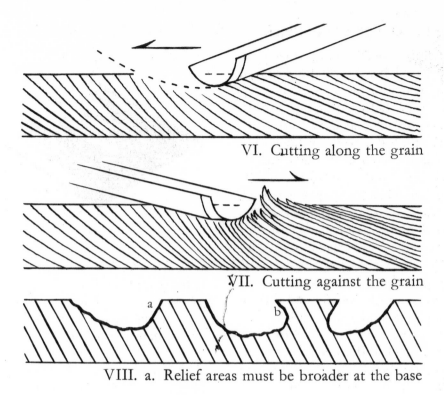

VI. Cutting along the grain

VII. Cutting against the grain

VIII. a. Relief areas must be broader at the base

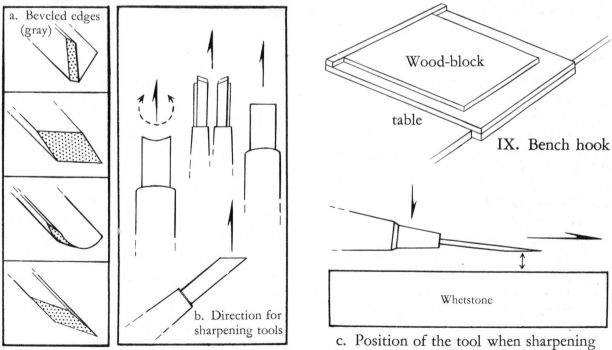

a. Beveled edges
(gray)

b. Direction for
sharpening tools

Wood-block

table

IX. Bench hook

Whetstone

c. Position of the tool when sharpening

X. Guide for sharpening tools

Transferring the Design to the Block

Because a design or drawing traced directly on the wood block will be reversed when printed from the block, the drawing is usually reversed before tracing it onto the block. There are several ways to do this, but one of the simplest is to draw the design on semitransparent paper with black ink so that the black lines will show through the back of the paper when the paper is turned over. Then place carbon paper face down upon the wood block, lay the design face down over the carbon paper and trace with pencil (over the lines showing through the back of the paper) those forms to be carved in the block. Remove the tracing and carbon paper and then apply India ink, with pen or brush, to the lines traced on the block. A wash of diluted black India ink can then be brushed over the block. This wash will darken the block and serve to contrast the carved and uncarved portions of the block during the carving.

Registry

Registry means the exact placing of successive colors as they are printed over each other. Three methods can be used to register the print paper on the wood block. The simplest method is to center the paper on the block by "eye." This method is recommended for the one-color print only. Lay the prepared block (one that has been carved and coated with printing media) on a flat surface. Center the paper (being sure to leave an adequate margin on the print paper) over the block and print. With this method, however, it is difficult to replace the paper on the block once the paper has been removed or to register it for a second color.

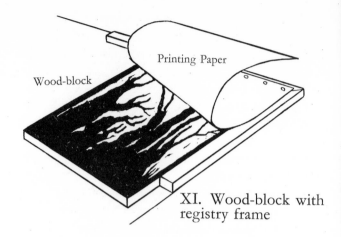

XI. Wood-block with registry frame

A second, more reliable method is to make a registry frame (XI) using two strips of wood about 3 inches wide and 15 inches long. Construct a right angle with the strips and attach it to the right corner of the table that will be used for printing. The frame should be slightly less thick than the wood block. Tack the printing paper along the right edge of the frame and slide the prepared block into the angle made by the frames; lower the paper onto the block and print.

If more than one block is used, one of two procedures can be followed. In the first procedure, the printed paper is removed and another paper tacked in place and printed. When enough copies from the first block are printed, the second block is placed in the frame and printed upon the paper over the previous color. In the second procedure, the print paper is left tacked to the frame, and the second prepared block is placed in the frame. With this procedure, the paper is taken off the frame only when the print is completed.

Note that in the "eye" centering method, the margins of the paper extend past the block. In the frame method, the margins of

14

the print paper rest on the registry frame. In both registry methods described, the print paper is larger than the wood block.

The third registry method, that of the Japanese *kento,* requires a wood block larger than the size of the print paper used. To make the *kento,* or registry guides, center and tack the drawing or design paper (on which the *kento* marks have been drawn to mark the left bottom edge and right lower corner of the print paper) on the block and trace the *kento* onto the block. Remove the paper from the block and make a straight cut along the traced *kento* lines with a Japanese knife on the wood block. Then use a flat chisel to carve a sloping depression inclined toward the cut in which to register the paper. Note: The *kento* lines (XIIa,b) should be positioned as far from the print area of the block as the width of the margin planned for the print.

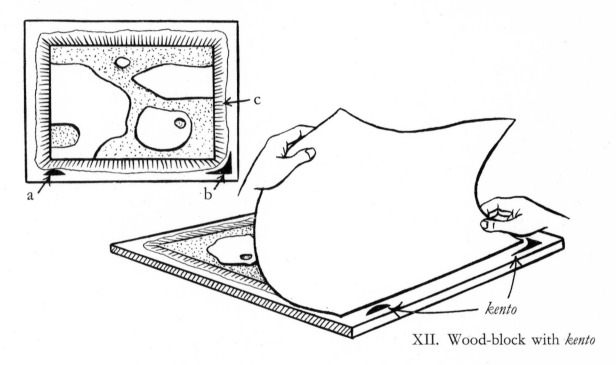

XII. Wood-block with *kento*

Paper

In Japan, traditional, handmade papers are called *wa-shi*; mechanically produced papers are called *yo-shi*. (The suffix *shi* means paper.) Papers for the *hanga* print are almost invariably made by the *wa-shi* method. Four kinds of plant material, each with certain characteristics, are used—singly or in combination—to form the *wa-shi* print papers:

Kozo (*Broussonetia kajinoki*), which has a strong, malleable, absorbent fiber; *mitsumata* (*Edgeworthia papyrifera*), which offers a softer, absorbent fiber; *gampi* (*Wickstroemia shikokiana*), which has a strong, fine but less absorbent fiber; and western wood pulp (coniferous woods), which is the least absorbent of the four materials but which helps to make paper thick, soft and pliable. The binder for good quality *wa-shi* paper comes

15

from a vegetable material known as *tororo-aoi* (*Hibiscus Manihot*). Papers made with this binder are uniform in thickness and will not affect the color of the completed print.

Pure *kozo* forms such excellent papers as *kozo-shi* and *kizuki-hosho*. *Kozo* is used, occasionally mixed with a small amount of wood pulp, for another good paper, *nishi-no-uchi*. *Kozo* is also used, mixed with varying percentages of wood pulp, to form softer papers referred to as *hosho-shi*. The two other plant materials, *mitsumata* and *gampi* are combined to form a paper called *torinoko*. Although this particular paper can be used for printing, it is generally considered too thin-bodied. A variation, *hanga torinoko,* combines *mitsumata, gampi* and coniferous wood pulp to form a thicker paper. It is available in large sheets, approximately 3 × 6 feet. (The label "rice paper," widely used in the West to designate Japanese papers, is meaningless in Japan and of little value elsewhere, for it makes no distinctions among the several papers.) All print paper has a face and a reverse. Although the face, or smoother side, is customarily used for the printing surface, some artists prefer the rougher reverse side.

The proper kind of paper is of prime importance, and selecting one involves consideration of color, flexibility, thickness, absorbency and presence (or absence) of size. This latter is important, for size gives controlled absorbency and strengthens the paper as well. (Presized Japanese papers are termed *dosa*, e.g., *dosa-kizuki-hosho*.) Paper can be tested for presence of size by placing a drop of water on its surface. If the water spreads and is absorbed completely, the paper has not been sized. If the drop retains its shape but leaves a damp spot when wiped off, the paper has been sized. If none of the water

is absorbed, the paper has been waterproofed with some substance other than size. Such paper is not, of course, suitable for a print method that will require an absorbent paper.

If the paper is not properly sized, it will be necessary to size it before printing. (An exception to this requirement is when the blotting and running effect of color upon the unsized paper is desirable.) A traditional Japanese size can be prepared in this way: obtain the following materials—180 cc. cold water, 3.75 grams dry glue (*nikawa* or rabbit glue), 1.12 grams of alum (during warm weather) or .80 grams of alum (during the colder season). Then soak the dry glue in cold water until the glue softens and increases in bulk. Heat the mixture carefully until the glue dissolves. Never allow it to boil as this will destroy the strength of the glue. Remove the glue from the heat. Add powdered alum and mix. Strain the glue mixture through a silk cloth. The size should be used while it is warm and it should be brushed evenly on the front of each sheet of paper. If the paper requires more sizing, brush sizing on the reverse side of the paper. If still more is required, brush the front side again. Once the hand-sized paper has dried completely, it may be handled like other papers. (Size spoils quickly, so prepare only the amount needed.)

Before printing with a water-soluble medium, the paper is usually dampened. One of several methods is to brush water onto each sheet and then stack the paper with alternate sheets of newspaper. Another method is to stack two or three sheets of paper to one sheet of blotter paper. Wrap the stack in a sheet of vinyl or plastic and let it soak from 10 minutes to 24 hours, depending upon the amount of saturation that is desired. If the paper is left too long, however, it will mildew.

Hand-printing oil-base media generally requires dry paper. (Lithograph and etching methods call for a dampened paper, but the pressure of the printing press is so great that the water is squeezed out of the paper and the oil pigment pressed in.)

Printing Materials

Both water-soluble and oil-base media are available for wood-block printing. Transparent watercolors, opaque tempera and *gouache, bokuju* (Japanese carbon ink in liquid form), *sumi* (Japanese carbon ink in stick form), India ink, dyes and a type of water-base printer's ink are the most commonly used water-soluble media. Commonly used oil-base media include the artist's oil colors as well as commercially produced printer's inks. (It is also possible to experiment with the newer "plastic paints.")

All water-soluble media (with the exception of the water-base printer's ink) are applied to the block with a brush. The Japanese have developed a variety of brushes that are excellent for this purpose.

Shoji-baké, a brush set into a wide handle (rabbit or badger hair) (XIIIa)
Burashi, a brush without a handle (horsehair) (XIIIb)
Penki-haké, a brush with an angled handle (rabbit or badger hair) (XIIIc)
Te-baké, a brush with a straight handle (horse, ox or pig bristle) (XIIId)
Abura-e-burashi, a western-type oil-painting brush (ox bristles) (XIIIe)
Fudé, a Japanese writing brush with a bamboo handle (rabbit or badger hair) (XIIIf)

The *te-baké* is the most important, and it is advisable to have several types and sizes of this brush. (Commonly available sizes range from .5 centimeters to 5 centimeters in width.) To use the *te-baké* correctly, hold the handle upright and give the brush a circular, scrubbing motion. Use the stiffer type of *te-baké* for applying thinner media to the block and the softer *te-baké* for heavier media.

To apply media properly to the block, dip a *te-baké* in water and brush the surface of the wood. Then dip another *te-baké* into the prepared media and apply it to the block, being careful to avoid filling the carved-out areas. (If the negative areas do fill, clean them out before printing the paper.) If more than one color is to be applied to the block (on separate forms) use another *te-baké*.

Use the *burashi* for applying media to broad areas of the block or for the initial

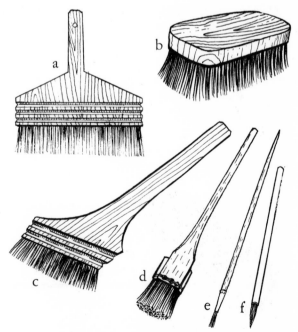

XIII. Wood-block printing brushes

dampening of the wood and the *penki-haké* for rewetting the margins of the print paper during the printing process. Use the western brush for fine or linear details and the *fudé* for the application of thin media to incised lines. The *shoji-baké* can be used for applying *dosa* and for wetting the paper before printing.

Both the *te-baké* and the *burashi* require special care to keep the bristles in condition. The Japanese artist uses a dried, tautly stretched sharkskin to split the ends of the bristles (see page 99). A coarse sandpaper, although inferior for splitting the bristles, will fray the ends somewhat.

Oil-base media are applied with rollers (also called brayers) that are available in various diameters, widths and qualities (XIV). Two types of rollers are generally used for wood-block printing—the gelatin and the hard rubber.

When artist's oils are used as the printing media, it may be necessary to remove the excess oil by putting the amount of paint to be used on absorbent paper. After some of the oil has been absorbed, scoop the paint onto a slab of heavy plate glass. (The slab should be large enough to allow free movement of the roller.) Roll the roller back and

forth on the paint until the surface of the roller is charged, or coated evenly with the paint. Discharge, or roll the paint onto the surface of the block, being careful not to fill in the carved, negative areas.

Commercial printer's inks are treated much like the artist's oils. Some of these inks may, however, require a small amount of linseed oil. The amount of oil must be gauged accurately, for too much oil will stain the print paper. Thoroughly mix the ink and linseed oil on the plate glass before charging the roller.

The effect produced by the oil-based media will depend in part on the type of roller used to apply them. The gelatin roller, for example, is a sensitive roller, with a pliant surface that can discharge media onto the lower textural areas of the block. But this roller must be used carefully, for a very soft gelatin roller can press the medium into areas where it is not wanted and so spoil the print. The other roller, the hard rubber type, has an insensitive surface and cannot discharge media evenly if the surface of the block is warped or uneven. (Some artists exploit the unevenness of the wood to achieve special effects in the print.)

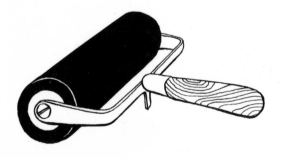

XIV. Roller

XV. *Baren*

Printing the Block

Place a felt pad, or similar device, under the prepared block to prevent slipping. Register the paper; smooth it from the center toward each corner. Place a second, thinner paper on top of the print to protect it. (Some handmade papers, although tough, have a tendency to "pull off" in layers when rubbed.)

Put a light coat of fine oil on the printing surface of the *baren*, a round pad made of paper and bamboo materials, used to apply pressure to the back of the print (XV). Grasp the *baren* in one hand. Starting at one section of the print, exert downward pressure and simultaneously move the *baren* in a circular movement over the print. Continue until the entire print has been rubbed with the *baren*. (Many weights of *baren* are used, for the texture of the coil in the *baren* produces a variety of effects in the printing. The heel of the hand exerts the pressure, not the knuckles. Note: Periodically rotate the inner coil of the *baren* to promote even wear.)

At this point, it is advisable to inspect the print. Weigh down one-half of the print and carefully roll back the other half. If the print appears weak, lower the paper and apply more pressure. Inspect again. If the print is still not satisfactory, then reapply media to the block where needed. Print again, and repeat for the other half of the print.

If upon initial inspection, it appears that the media was applied too heavily to the block and pushed down into the carved lines, remove the paper. Clean the block thoroughly and start over with a fresh sheet of paper.

For multicolor prints, prepare the paper for a second printing. If the medium is transparent watercolor, dye or carbon ink, stack each printed sheet between dampened blotter sheets and wrap in the sheet of vinyl. While printing, dampen the margins occasionally to avoid uneven drying and subsequent shrinking of the margins.

Tempera or *gouache,* if applied thickly, will have to dry before the second printing. Redampen the paper from the back. Oil-based inks or artist's oil colors usually have to dry also between printings. (Printing wet on wet is sometimes done so that the over-printed colors will merge.)

Signing the Print

The standard information required on the bottom margin of the print is as follows: the title, sequence number and edition limit, artist's signature, and date. The "sequence number" is the numerical order in which the print was made—1, 2, 3, etc., and the "edition limit" refers to the arbitrary number of prints that are to be made—5, 10, 25, etc. (7/50 is the seventh print made of an edition limited to 50 copies. 50/50 indicates that the edition has been completed. AP means Artist's Proof.) Prints without any numbering are usually unlimited editions.

Recording the Data

Print techniques and facts need to be recorded. Get a notebook for the pertinent data concerning each print. State the number of blocks and their printing sequence. (Also label the blocks themselves.) Make color swatches for each color with notes on how and what colors were mixed. Note any unusual or special techniques utilized, write down the title, edition limit, number made, sold, etc. Include a sketch of the print as a reminder.

II. Specific Applications

This section is designed to be used with the section which introduced the basic methods for making wood-block prints. To avoid repetition, information covered in the previous section will be repeated only when necessary to clarify a particular detail. The beginner will get best results if he uses the first application before trying others. After he has mastered it and worked with all the applications—each produces effects of distinct character and style—he can make interesting combinations of these basic processes.

The Single-Color Block

This technique uses the positive or relief surface of the block for receiving the print media. The negative, or cutaway areas of the block, do not receive color.

After designing the print and choosing the registry method, transfer the design to the block. (The design can also be drawn directly on the block.) Cover the block with a wash of black ink and designate the negative areas with white paint, or paint the block with white poster paint and designate the positive areas with black ink. In either case, remove the white areas when carving.

After carving the block, clean off the wood particles. Choose the medium, apply color to

XVI. Single color block

the block, register the prepared paper, and print. (See Kihei Sasajima, page 46, plate 20; Shiko Munakata, page 45, plate 19; Un'ichi Hiratsuka, page 52, plate 30.)

Two Colors with a Key Block

This technique produces a multicolored print by utilizing one block for the main portion of the design; this block, the key block, is usually printed black. The other block(s) are used for the supporting portion(s) or color(s).

These interrelated blocks can be designed in two ways: One way is to, make the drawing for the key block, then lay tracing paper over the drawing. Trace just the supporting portions. Decide on registry. Reverse both the key block design and the supporting design(s) before tracing them onto the blocks. Both sides of the block may be used if the block is thick enough. Trace the design(s) and carve the blocks. The other way is to design the key block on paper, reverse the design and transfer onto the key block. Carve. Print several copies from the key block (XVIIa). Use the print from the key block as a basis for determining the color areas of the supporting block(s) (XVIIb). Decide on registry. Reverse the design before transferring it to the second block. Carve.

Determine which block is to be printed first. If the key block is printed first, the print will be modified by the overprinting of the second block; therefore, it is customary to print the key block last (XVIIc). (See Kiyoshi Saito, page 50, plate 26.)

Two Colors without a Key Block

This approach requires two or more blocks, each of which have equal importance in the composition of the design. Make the design in the colors that will be used for the print. Lay tracing paper over the completed design and trace the form(s) that will be used for the first block (XVIIIa). Each form must be a separate unit. Lay a second tracing paper over the painted design and trace the remaining forms that will be used for the second block (XVIIIb). Decide on the registry. Reverse and transfer the two designs onto the respective blocks. Carve and print (XVIIIc).

Note: Colors can be applied to different forms on the same block if they are self-contained, separated forms. Using more than one color on a single block offers the possibility of a number of colors from only two blocks. For best results apply colors to the block with a brush. (See Gen Yamaguchi, page 49, plate 24 and Haku Maki, page 51, plate 28.)

XVII. a. The key-block print   b. The supporting block print   c. The completed print

Printing on Dark Papers

With this technique, which requires only a linear design, the carving is quick and simple, but the printing is complicated. Because the printing paper is black, the carved-out areas will also be black in the print. The remaining relief forms are colored and then printed on the black paper.

To darken the paper, brush unsized paper with carbon ink and allow to dry. Brush sizing on the now black paper and allow to dry. Dampen the prepared paper before printing.

If possible, use a registry frame with this technique. Use a bold line for the design, reverse and transfer it to the block. Use a Japanese knife or a veiner to carve out the lines. The lines must be clean-cut and fairly deep. Use tempera or *gouache* color. Prepare white and other colors to a consistency of cream and keep in small dishes. Dampen the block, put a small amount of thin paste onto the surface and use a printer's brush to apply white paint. White is usually printed first and the block cleaned. The other colors are then applied to the block and printed over the white forms on the dark paper. (Printing the colors directly will result in their being absorbed by the dark paper with a consequent loss of brilliance.) In this technique, use a light pressure when rubbing with the *baren*.

If a registry frame is not used, lift only part of the paper and apply other colors to the block. Print the paper again. If the paper dries, dampen it from the back. Be sure to record the printing data for this monoprint-like technique. (See Tadashige Ono, page 38, color plate 8.)

The Embossed Print

Carved blocks are often works of art in themselves. The color print produced from the block does not as a rule express the bas-relief design of the wood itself. Artists seeking a way to express the beauty of the block have used the embossing technique—which is ordinarily used only in combination with

 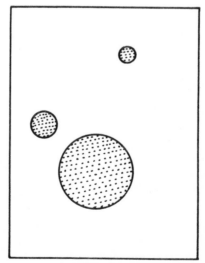 

XVIII. a. Block one   b. Block two   c. Print from blocks one and two

other techniques to make color prints—to create prints without color. (See Haku Maki, page 51, plate 28.)

Use a very sturdy, highly sized *torinoko* paper. Thoroughly dampen the paper, wrap it in a sheet of vinyl and let it stand for about 24 hours.

The design for the block may be built up in relief, or carved into the block or both. Wire, heavy cord, slender sticks of wood, sand, etcetera, may also be glued to the block to build up a relief surface. Register the damp paper onto the block. Then, using a slender tool that has a smooth, rounded end, such as a burnisher or orange stick, (various sizes may be needed) press the paper around the forms in relief and into the form cut or incised into the block (see 52, page 71). (The embossing can have either a raised or reverse character.) Work slowly and deliberately until the print is completed. Hang the print to dry. Drying the print flat may cause some of the embossed areas to sink and become flat.

Plastic Print

This spontaneous technique is becoming more popular among the contemporary printers either as a technique complete in itself or as one used in combination with other techniques.

Although the design can be planned, this technique, building up a relief surface, encourages a more flexible, spontaneous use of the materials directly on the block itself.

Cut to size and brush shellac on a piece of plywood for the foundation. (The shellac will seal the wood and make it easier to clean.) Then build up the block surface by applying polymer or vinyl paints, shellac,

XIX. Plastic print

lacquer, glue—anything that will adhere to the surface of the block and dry hard—to produce a relief texture or surface. The materials can be dripped, spattered, brushed, combed, formed into plastic patterns, and so forth, to form a variety of interesting effects. The applied materials must be thoroughly dried or the relief surface made by the material may come off onto the paper when pressure is applied by the *baren* during the printing. Register the paper and print. For best results use rollers to apply the printing medium to the block. Register the paper and print. (See Hiroyuki Tajima, pages 39, 42, color plates 11, 16.)

Combine Print

The combine print is made by gluing or impressing various textured objects on the block. It may include gluing leaves, netting, textured papers, string, sand, etcetera, or, for example, hammering objects, such as heavy wire mesh, on the block to impress the texture into the wood. Anything that will make an impression, or texture, in the block or produce a relief effect on the surface of the block can be used.

First, glue or impress the objects onto the block, or both. Objects glued to the surface of the block should be as thin as possible. Too high a relief will raise the printing paper away from the surrounding areas and cause the paper to rip or tear. Register the paper and print. An oil-base medium applied with a roller is best for this technique, although it may be printed with water-base paint as was done in Reika Iwami's print. (See plate 23, page 48.)

Subtractive Print

This technique is used for effectively lightening or subtracting color from the print by means of a bleach. The technique must be used in combination with other techniques. (See the light, floating forms in Stone Flower, Red page 33, color plate 1.)

Make a drawing of the areas of the print that will be bleached. Trace these forms on a sturdy, absorbent paper, remembering the need to reverse the forms, and then cut the forms out. Glue the forms onto the block. Brush a household chlorine bleach onto the paper forms now glued to the block, register the print paper, and "print" with the *baren*. Lift the print paper off the block. Brush distilled white vinegar on the paper forms on the block and on the now bleached areas of the print. After several minutes have passed, blot the bleached forms with a blotter. The vinegar will neutralize the destructive action of the chlorine. Note: The print paper will eventually deteriorate if not neutralized in this way.

The Baren

The *baren* is a unique tool developed specifically for use in the Japanese method of manual printing. Contemporary print artists, though not sure of the origin of this tool or even of the exact meaning of the written characters for the word *baren*, generally believe that the idea for such a tool came from China about a thousand years ago. The Japanese *baren*, made of bamboo husks and dry lacquer, differs, however, from the early Chinese version, which was made of "soft materials"—similar perhaps to those in the tampon or dauber now used for stone rubbing. The Japanese *baren* may also have been influenced by an early Korean tool for applying pressure to prints. This device consisted of a block wrapped with horse hair. The surmise of Korean influence is strengthened by the correlation between the Korean character for "horse" and the Japanese character for "*ba*" in *baren*.

Whatever its exact source, the *baren* of today is the same as that used four hundred years ago, for the printers have passed on the details of its construction from master to apprentice.

One of the few remaining printer-craftsmen who possess the skill and knowledge to make a traditional *baren* is Shokichi Kobayashi. As the craftsmen have for many years, he makes the traditional *baren*, which consists of three parts: the *baren* proper, a flat spiral or coil made from a tough, nubbed cord twisted from bamboo-husk fibers; the *ategawa*, a shallow, walled disc made from laminated paper; and the *takenogawa* or *barengawa*, a combined printing surface and grip formed from a single bamboo husk. To make this traditional *baren*, Kobayashi prepares the materials for the three parts, makes the parts, and then assembles the completed parts to form the *baren*.

Kobayashi explains that he begins by preparing the bamboo husks. He uses husks from a species of bamboo found in Kyushu,

1

Japan. He chose this particular bamboo because it does not have the spot-forming pigment that weakens the tensile strength of the fibers. He cleans the husks by soaking them in water for 10 to 14 days, during which time he changes the water daily to prevent the husks from turning sour. Then he air-dries them, and stores them until he needs them.

When he is ready to make the cord for a *baren,* Kobayashi selects a number of these prepared bamboo husks. Then, seating himself on the floor, Japanese-style, he proceeds. He first dampens the husks with a wet cloth. Then, using a single-bladed knife, he cuts the husks into one-inch strips. He places a single strip upon a smooth surface and scrapes the inner, fleshy part away with a flat-edged knife; next, he slices the one-inch strips into many narrow strands (2). Kobayashi paused at this point to explain that the traditional method of cutting took

considerable time and care, as a single-bladed knife was meticulously used to cut each slender strand. To hasten this process, he has ingeniously fashioned a comb-like cutter from his wife's sewing needles. He is now able to cut several strands at a time and can control the thickness of the fiber strands by gauging the set of the needles. He has made several such tools, and has attached a sample of finished *baren* cord to each tool as a reference to the set of the needles. Kobayashi then takes two of the narrow strands and prepares to wind the cord. First he ties the two strands together and secures them by driving an awl through the knot to fix it to his workbench. Next, he takes one strand in each hand, holding it between his thumb and forefinger, and twists the strands clockwise around each other (3). When Kobayashi nears the end of the strands, he ties on additional strands. He continues to twist and add new strands until he has about forty

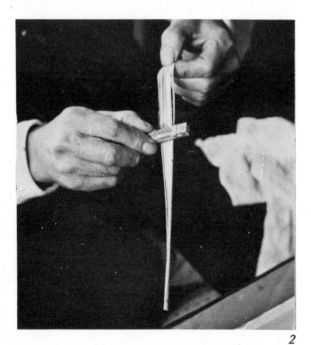

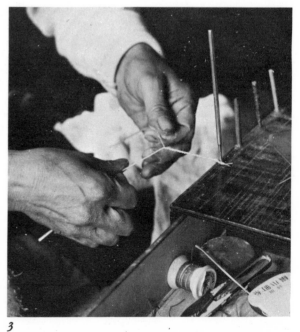

2

3

meters of cord. He takes up the increasing length by winding the completed cord, figure-8 fashion, around three pegs attached to the bench. After he has made the full length, he winds the 2-ply cord on a spool.

Since *baren* are usually made from 8-ply, 12-ply, or 16-ply cord, Kobayashi combines the 2-ply strands to make the necessary thicknesses. He twists two 2-ply cords together counterclockwise to form a 4-ply cord. To make an 8-ply cord, he twists together two 4-ply cords, reversing the direction of the twisting (4). To make a 12-ply cord, he combines a 4-ply cord and an 8-ply cord. And to make a 16-ply cord, he combines a 4-ply cord and a 12-ply cord (Two 8-ply cords can be used, but they are more difficult to twist together tightly); throughout he reverses the direction of twisting. When he has the desired thickness of cord, Kobayashi trims the cord with scissors to remove the wisps and ends of

the bamboo fibers and wraps the completed cord around a cylinder to impart a natural spring. It should be noted that the final size of the cord's diameter does not depend only upon the number of ply used but also upon the initial thickness of the bamboo strand. Because of the care he has taken in cutting the strands, however, Kobayashi is able to make a "standard" size cord.

Kobayashi next forms the spiral, an operation in which he must use his teeth as well as his hands. He begins by forming a circular loop at one end of the cord and binding the loop securely with four long, doubled threads, the ends of which will later be used to tie the segments of the spiral together. He coils the cord around and around to form the flat spiral, tying the segments together at quarter rotations (with the threads which he holds between his teeth when they are not needed) until two-thirds of the spiral is completed. He then adds four

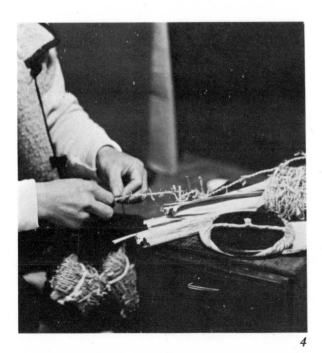

4   5

more threads and ties the remainder of the spiral at one-eighth turns (5). He makes the last two segments of the spiral from twisted paper cord which is of the same thickness as the bamboo cord. He uses the paper cord for the outer circumference because the harsh bamboo cord would damage the laminated paper disc which houses the *baren*.

This laminated paper disc, the *ategawa*, is the "shell" which holds the *baren* spiral. A properly made *ategawa* has several subtle but important characteristics. It must be flexible but sturdy, light but durable, thin but not subject to warping. It must also be made so that it is thicker in the middle than at the circumference. Kobayashi is able to make an *ategawa* which meets these requirements only by laminating paper. He prefers to use the *kozo* paper used in books published some thirty years ago, for he feels this paper is better for the laminating process than recently made papers.

Kobayashi begins to make the *ategawa* by cutting out five circles, each of a specific type of paper and a specific diameter. The largest circle, which is referred to as No. 1, measures about $8\frac{1}{4}$ inches in diameter and is of a pure *kozo* paper. No. 2, also of *kozo*, measures $5\frac{1}{4}$ inches. Nos. 3 and 4, measuring $4\frac{3}{4}$ inches and $3\frac{1}{2}$ inches respectively, are of a heavier paper called *shojigami*. The smallest circle, No. 5, is $2\frac{1}{2}$ inches in diameter and is of *kozo* paper. In all, Kobayashi uses forty circles in the following sequence: 1-1-1-1-1-1-1-1-2-2-1-1-2-2-1-1-2-2-1-1-3-2-4-5-1-1-2-3-2-1-1-2-2-1-1-1-1-1-1.

Kobayashi must place the paper circles on a polished wooden form that will give them their final shape. After wetting the form, Kobayashi dampens the first layer of paper and places it carefully on the form. He places the succeeding layers, each brushed over with a thin rice paste, one by one upon the form at two- to five-day intervals, depending upon the dampness of the weather. During this

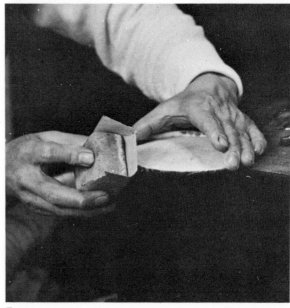

6   7

process, he takes great care to place each circle so that the grain of the paper does not run parallel to that of the preceding paper circles; this difference in the position of the grains effectively counters warping. The last layer he applies is made of thin silk fabric. Then, after the *ategawa* has been thoroughly dried, Kobayashi coats it with lacquer, which waterproofs it and gives it beauty.

Almost a year from the day that he placed the first layer of paper on the wooden form, Kobayashi gently pries the *ategawa* loose from the wooden form. He trims the circumference to the proper height, which is slightly less than the height of the *baren* spiral, using a knife that rests upon a support of three old Japanese coins (6). Then he sands the cut edge (7) and adds the date and craftman's seal; the *ategawa* is now ready for the final step of covering.

Before he begins this final step, Kobayashi prepares the *barengawa*. He first moistens a large bamboo husk and then smooths it with his hands. Next, he softens and stretches the husk by lightly crushing the fibers with a tool made from old Japanese coins (8). Then, centering the *ategawa*, which has been "stuffed" with the cord spiral, upon the inner side of the husk (9) and taking care to leave sufficient margins, he uses scissors to taper the husk's ends, which are to be formed into a grip.

Now he is ready for the crucial step in completing the *baren*, the folding of the edges of the husk over the circular *ategawa*. He must exercise great care in this step, for the underside, the surface that will be applied to the print, must be flat and taut. He starts this step by making successive folds in the one edge of the husk, from the center to one end. Then he makes successive folds in the opposite edge of the same half of the husk; this half of the husk now fits snugly around the *ategawa*. Kobayashi tightly twists the tapered end and holds it firmly in one hand while he makes folds in the second half of the husk and fits it to the *ategawa* (10). He then lays the twisted ends across the

8

9

10

11

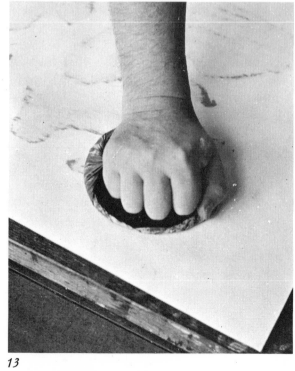

12

13

lacquered back (11) of the *ategawa* and firmly binds them in place with twine (12). Finally, Kobayashi lightly coats the printing surface with camellia oil. This oiling must be done before and after each printing session to prevent the husk from becoming dry and brittle and to facilitate the movement of the *baren* across the paper during printing (13).

Occasionally, artists design their own *baren*, to satisfy either their curiosity or an individual need, e.g., Hagiwara's *baren* made from an electric stove element. Hodaka Yoshida has experimented with various weights of sandpaper, and Kidokoro has used a flat, untextured circle of veneer. Tajima, interestingly, has improvised a *baren* reminiscent of the early Korean ones by wrapping heavy twine around a block of wood which has first been coated with glue. Not all wood-block artists, of course, design their own *baren*, but each of them is able to cover the *baren*—the *barengawa* or cover must be replaced periodically, the other two parts are permanent—and usually keeps a supply of bamboo husks for the purpose. No satisfactory substitute for the bamboo husk has yet been discovered. Since the *baren* is of prime importance to the artists, they tend to feel that the caliber of the artist can be judged by his *baren*. They say, among themselves, that a properly covered *baren* shows the general professional skill of the artist, while an overall wearing out of the *baren's* printing surface, and the absence of calluses on the artist's knuckles show that the artist knows how to use his *baren*.

But these artists are not the only ones who use *baren*, for there are other people, amateurs and students, who make wood-block prints. For these people, who ordinarily do not need or want expensive, handcrafted equipment, there are cheaper, mass-produced *baren*. The cheapest *baren* are made solely from twisted paper, which is usually waterproofed with the juice of a nonedible persimmon. The paper-cord *baren* is not tied with string but is merely coated with glue so that the segments adhere to each other. A better, but still comparatively inexpensive *baren* is made from two lengths of twisted hemp which are twisted together and then formed into a spiral and placed upon a sturdy disc of paper that has been coated with glue. In these cheaper *baren*, the *ategawa* is a modification of that made by Kobayashi, in which fewer sheets and heavier paper are used. The simplest *ategawa* is only a disc of plain or corrugated cardboard. These simpler, mass-produced *baren* are not nearly so refined or long-lasting as those made by Kobayashi, but they are passable tools with which to apply pressure to the print.

Kobayashi prefers to make the traditional *baren* despite the great time and care it requires. He does, however, occasionally make substitute *baren* on demand. He is often asked, for example, to make a *baren* of two-ply copper wire twisted into shape with pliers and secured by thin wire. The making of the traditional *baren* is not a lucrative occupation, but Kobayashi's pride in being one of the few remaining craftsmen in a long tradition of craftsmanship helps to sustain him. So great is his dedication to his craft that, despite its drawbacks, he intends to teach his craft to his only son so that the tradition may continue for yet a while.

List of Illustrations

Pl.1.
Hideo Hagiwara
Stone Flower, Red
1960   23" × 34¼"

Pl.2. Tadashi Nakayama *Horse* 1960 *24″ × 18 ½″*

Pl.3. Rokushu Mizufune *Drifting* 1963 *29 ½″ × 13 ½″*

Pl.4.
Fumio Kitaoka
Iso (*A*)   1962
$21\frac{3}{4}'' \times 33\frac{1}{2}''$

Pl.5.
Sho Kidokoro
*Apocalypse,
Vermilion*
1963 $22\frac{3}{4}'' \times 16''$

Pl.6.   Hodaka Yoshida   *Sato*   1964   *25″ × 13″*

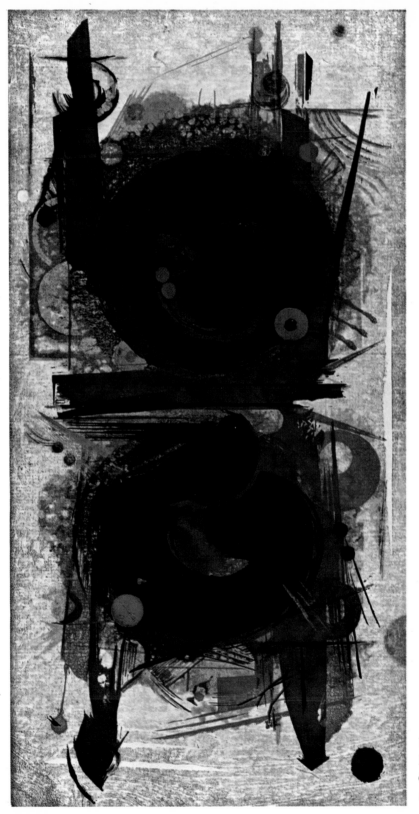

Pl.7.
Hodaka Yoshida
Offering, B 1962
$14\frac{3}{4}'' \times 29\frac{1}{2}''$

Pl.8.
Tadashige Ono
Riverbank, Tokyo
1955   6″ × 3¾″

Pl.9.
Umetaro Azechi *Mountain Man in White* 1964   10″ × 12¼″

Pl.10.
Jun-ichiro Sekino *Children's Faces* 1956   15¾″ × 20¾″

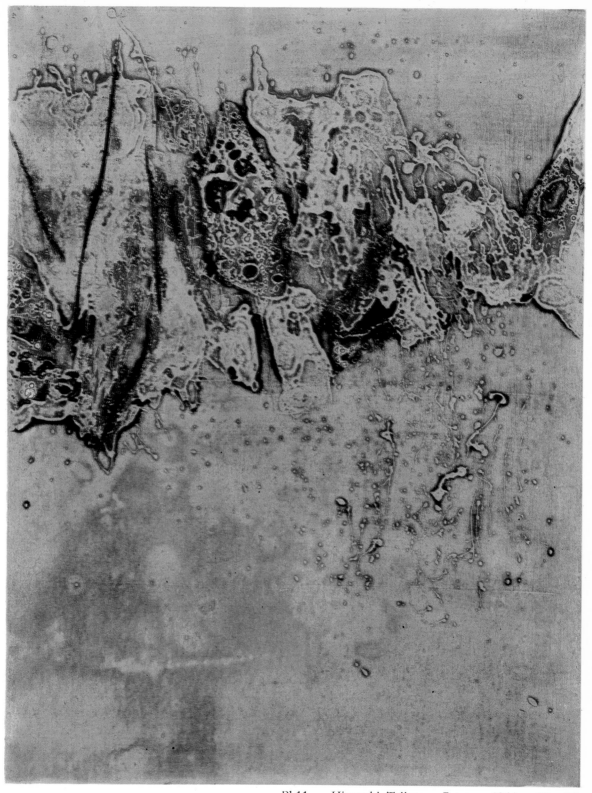

Pl.11. Hiroyuki Tajima *Popox* 1964 *18″×25″*

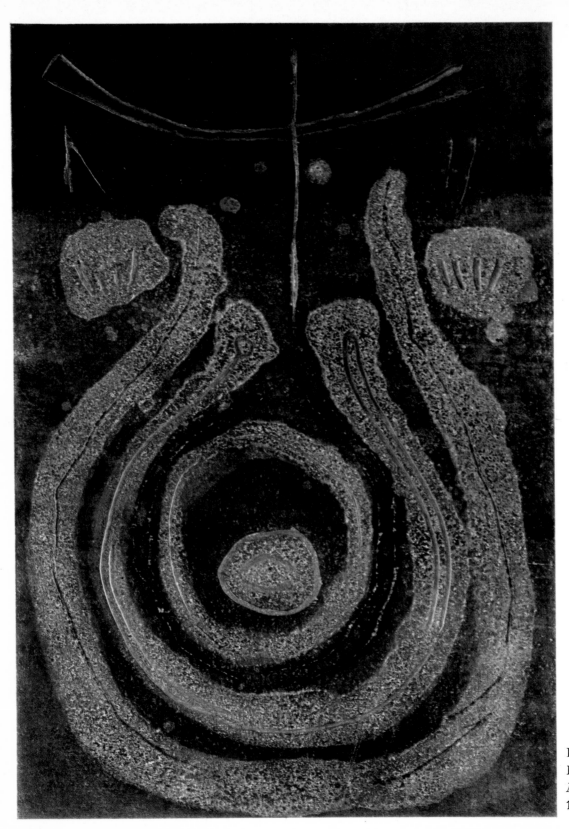

Pl.12.
Hideo Hagiwara
Mask No. 9
1964   *24½″ × 36″*

Pl.13.
Sho Kidokoro
Celebration
1964 $22\frac{3}{4}'' \times 15\frac{3}{4}''$

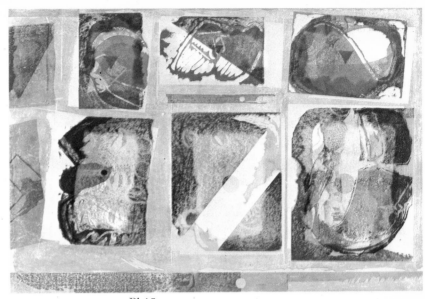

Pl.14.   Kazumi Amano   *Moral(Tai)*   1963 $18'' \times 24\frac{1}{8}''$

Pl.15.
R.G. Robertson   *Djuna's Night*   1964 $21'' \times 34''$

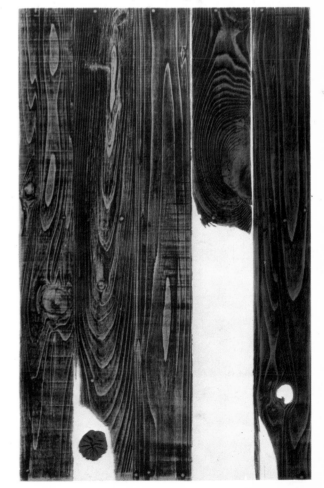

Pl.16.   Hiroyuki Tajima   *Benibe, B*   1961   *15″ × 19¾″*

Pl.17.
Joichi Hoshi
Constellation (1)
1965   *13⅛″ × 23″*

Pl.18.
Tokio Miyashita   *Work* (B)   1964   *11¼″×21″*

Pl.19.
Shiko Munakata
Zaō 1957
9″ × 12½″

Pl.20.
Kihei Sasajima
Woods 1955
6″ × 5″

Pl.21
Tomio Kinoshit
Kamen Tachi 1 195
35¾″ × 24

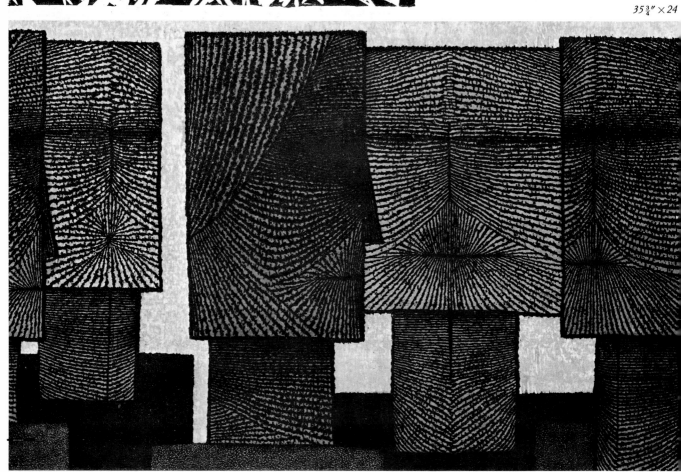

Pl.22.
Okiie Hashimoto
Stone and Sand Garden
1960 $20\frac{1}{2}'' \times 28\frac{3}{4}''$

Pl.23.　　Reika Iwami　*Ocean Series: Cloud Talk*　1962　*17″×23″*

Pl.24.   Gen Yamaguchi   *Composition Mo* $22\frac{1}{2}'' \times 28\frac{1}{4}''$

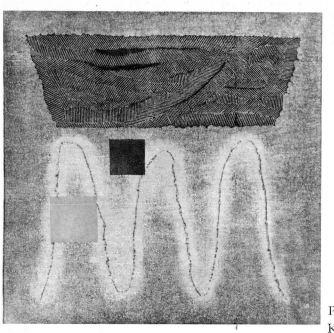

Pl.25.
Masaji Yoshida   *Kukan No. 28*   1963 $22\frac{1}{4}'' \times 22\frac{1}{4}''$

Pl.26.
Kiyoshi Saito   *White Porcelain*   1957 $23\frac{1}{2}'' \times 17\frac{3}{4}''$

Pl.27.
Shiro Takagi
Kurenai no Genso 1962
$31\frac{1}{2}'' \times 20\frac{3}{4}''$

Pl.28. Haku Maki *Composition 63-A* 1963 $15\frac{1}{2}'' \times 23\frac{3}{8}''$

Pl.29. Fumiaki Fukita *Cloud of Genius* 1965 $17\frac{1}{8}'' \times 24''$

Pl.30.
Un'ichi Hiratsuka
Koto Yoshun 1960
$16\frac{1}{8}'' \times 23\frac{3}{8}''$

Six Contemporary Printmakers

Umetaro Azechi

1902   Born, Ehime Pref., Shikoku, Japan.

1919–21 Sailor for two years.

1921   Moved to Tokyo. Studied Western art via a correspondence course.

1923   Was evacuated from Tokyo after the "great earthquake" to Shikoku. While there, painted signs for a movie theatre.

1925   Returned to Tokyo determined to become a painter. Found employment in a government printing plant where he made first prints by scratching pictures on soft lead plates.

1930   Met Un'ichi Hiratsuka, already a noted artist, who encouraged Azechi and suggested he exhibit his work in the Hanga Association Exhibit. One print in the exhibit was reproduced in the magazine *Mizue*.

1931–36 Exhibited oil paintings with the Haku Jitsu Kai and the Kokuga Kai. Content of work was primarily architectural scenes and later seascapes reminiscent of his native Shikoku. In a later exhibit organized by Hiratsuka, Azechi won a prize for his wood block, copies of which were sold, one to an imperial prince. This success resulted in his decision to give up oils and become a print artist. Developed wood-block technique while working as an artisan-printer for Hiratsuka and later Onchi and Maekawa. During this period he was attracted to the mountains and began making prints of them.

1950–65 Today Azechi makes his living not only from prints, but from designing magazine covers and similar commercial work, and from writing about the mountains and mountaineers that have become the subject of his art. Has exhibited prints in the Biennale, São Paulo, Biennale of Prints, Tokyo, and in numerous other exhibitions in Japan and the rest of the world. Lives in Tokyo. Member, Japan Print Association.

15

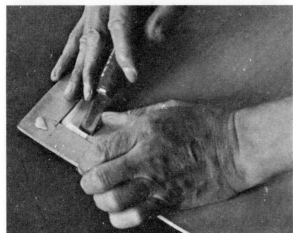

16

17

Preparing the Wood Blocks

First, Azechi makes a preliminary drawing on *wa-shi* paper with Pentel, a crayon similar to the oil pastels available in the West. Because he uses the Pentels thickly and because the long fibers of the paper have a tendency to unravel, he produces a texture similar to that of an oil painting. Azechi places a newspaper on the drawing several times and rubs over it with a *baren* to absorb the excess color.

Next, he cuts five blocks of plywood, three of $\frac{1}{4}$ inch *shina* veneer and two of $\frac{1}{8}$ inch *rawan*, to size for the carving. Then he traces the drawing for the carving in two steps. First, he lays a piece of carbon paper, carbon side up, on the table. Over this carbon, he places the drawing, face up, and traces over it to produce an image on the reverse side (15). Before he proceeds to the next step, he cuts registry marks or *kento* into the blocks, using the preliminary drawing as a guide (16). Azechi begins the second step by reexamining the drawing and making several changes. Next he puts carbon paper, carbon side down, on the blocks and places the drawing, face down, over the carbon.

18

Then he registers the drawing with the *kento*, thumbtacks it to the block, and traces those lines necessary to define the form for each printing sequence (17). Azechi does not consistently follow the original lines of the drawing but makes slight changes during the tracing. (He uses the two-step tracing method so that the image on the block will not be printed in reverse, which will happen if he traces the drawing directly.)

Now Azechi carves the *kento* on the remaining blocks (16). He cuts off the corners of each block to prevent the veneer from peeling, which sometimes happens if the plywood corners are bumped or frayed. Then he marks the title of the print and the year on the back of the blocks. (When he finishes the print and knows the exact sequence, he will add the number of the block.)

For the carving, Azechi uses traditional Japanese wood-block tools, a wood sculptor's chisel, and a shoemaker's knife (18). He sharpens all these tools repeatedly on a stone (*toishi*) during the carving (19). (The steel used in the Japanese tools is much softer than that used in Western tools; as a result, they can be sharpened quickly and easily.) The artist's carving methods for each block, as the photographs show, are similar.

First Block: (23) Azechi uses a V-shaped chisel or veiner to cut out the lines of the form that he has traced on the block. He chisels and peels off with a U-shaped gouge the first layer of the veneer between the edge of the block and the traced form. Then he uses the gouge to carve out a *Daruma*-shaped form that surrounds the circular shape in the center of the traced form (20). He employs a wide, flat chisel to clean and smooth out the areas that he has cut away. And he uses a knife to taper and soften the edges of

19

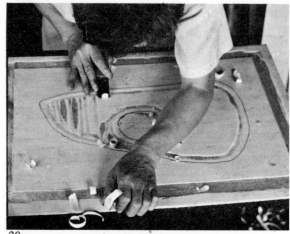
20

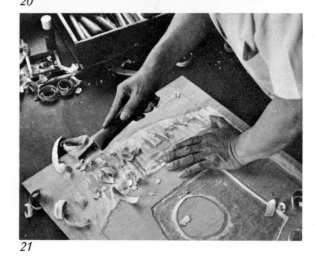
21

56

the shapes to avoid the sharp edges that would otherwise result in the printing. Finally, Azechi cuts a small circular shape in the bottom left area of the block where his *han* or signature mark will be printed.

Second Block: (24) Azechi uses the veiner again to cut around the traced form. He carves out the negative areas, parts to be cut away, just as he did with the first block. But he leaves the edges of the form sharply defined so that a hard edge will be produced in the print.

Third Block: (25) As he did for the first and second blocks, Azechi uses *shina*-faced plywood, with the grain running vertically to the picture plane, for block three. He uses the same carving methods for this block that he used for block two.

Fourth Block: (26) Azechi uses the *rawan* veneer, with the grain running vertically to contrast with the fifth block, which he will use with the grain running horizontally. (Because the two blocks overlapped in approximately the same areas of the print, the contrasting grain pattern formed an interest-

ing textural effect. Blocks with opposing or contrasting grain patterns are often used to exploit the netlike texture that results in the print at the point where the contrasting grain patterns overlap.)

He uses a small gouge to cut out the textured circular form in the center of the block. He cuts the outside of the large form just as he did in the previous blocks. Then he carves out the linear forms within the large shape with a small veiner. Finally, he carves his *han* into the bottom corner of the block.

Fifth Block: (27) Azechi carves the fifth block, which is *rawan* veneer with the grain running horizontally, in the same way he carved the fourth block (22). He makes many changes during the carving, for he is intuitively modifying the forms to create new images and ideas that gradually evolve as the work progresses. (In addition to the five blocks described, Azechi had previously carved four different versions of the blocks but had rejected them because he felt they did not work successfully in the print.) (21)

22   23   24

25   26   27

The Printing Process

Azechi uses a hand-sized *kozo* paper, *senka,* that is made in his native village. He cuts, then moistens it with a wide *shoji* makers' brush and allows it to soak between layers of blotting paper for about three hours. (Newspapers can be used in place of the blotting paper.) He chooses, as he usually does, to use the back of the paper for printing because it has a rough texture that he feels is suitable for his style of print.

First Color—Block one: First Azechi brushes water on the block and then sands it with a stone (*toishi*) to eliminate any slivers or surface roughness. Then he washes the block to remove the grit and wood particles.

(Wetting the block before applying the paint obviates the tendency of the dry wood to soak up the paint and cause an uneven printing. The block is sometimes used dry when a more textural or more surface effect is desired.)

Next Azechi squeezes paint out of tubes directly on the block. (He uses an opaque, Japanese watercolor, *Suisai Enogu,* for all the print sequences.) He mixes sky blue, viridian, and ivory black with the stiff brush traditionally used by Japanese printmakers and spreads the paint until it covers the block evenly. He thins the medium blue-gray mixture by adding water from a small teakettle.

(Colors are mixed directly on the block only for single prints or for first printings where some experimenting is necessary to determine what colors will be used. When many editions are printed at one time, colors are mixed in quantity in bowls.)

After Azechi brushes the color evenly over the block, he registers the corner and one side of the print paper in the *kento* and then places the print sheet on the block. He lays heavy brown wrapping paper, actually two sheets of wrapping paper between which cheesecloth has been glued or laminated, over the print and rubs with the *baren.* He uses the laminated paper to give more "tooth" to the *baren* and thereby impresses the color into the print paper more effectively. Next he places the print face up, lays newspaper on top of the print, and rubs again with the *baren* to pick up any excess moisture or pigment. Because he feels the first application of color is too weak, he prints again to deepen the color (color plate 31a).

Second Color—Block Two: Again applying paint directly to the block (29), Azechi brushes white pigment over the block and prints from it. Because he applies the paint thickly, he does not rub but taps the *baren* on the print with light, quick motions so that the paint is impressed more thickly on the paper (31). Then he blots the print, applies a second coat of white to the block, and prints again to make the color on the print more opaque (color plate 31b).

Third Color—Block One: Azechi mixes burnt sienna, yellow ochre and carmine red, applies the mixture to the circular form in the center of the first block, and prints using the same technique he used for the first color (color plate 31a).

Fourth Color—Block Three: He mixes sky blue, ivory black, and viridian on the dampened block to make a dark, muted blue and then prints from the block twice (color plate 31c).

Fifth Color—Block Four: Azechi mixes sky blue and ivory black and applies this mixture somewhat more thinly than he has the previous colors. He uses the same printing method as before, but this time he makes only one run. Finally he prints the small, circular *han* at the bottom of the block with the red he has used previously (color plate 31d).

28

29

Sixth Color—Block Five: He applies ivory black to the block and prints this color more opaquely than the fifth color but in the same manner. Because the margins of the print dry more rapidly than the printed areas, which are dampened with each printing, Azechi periodically brushes water on the margins. If the margins are not dampened regularly, they will dry and shrink and so alter the registry. (Color plates 31e, 31f.)

When he completes the printing process, he cleans the blocks with a damp rag to remove the paint. Then he stores them flat and places rocks on top of them to prevent warping.

The usual number of editions Azechi makes of each print is between fifty and eighty. Sometimes several years pass before an edition is complete because Azechi usually prints an initial ten copies and the remainder only upon demand. Occasionally he becomes dissatisfied with certain prints and destroys the blocks regardless of the number of editions printed or of their popularity. Most of his work is motivated by a single subject: mountains and mountaineers. He also writes about this subject for a variety of publications. When asked about the content of the print "Dark Footsteps," he replied that it was motivated by the snow blindness he had experienced while climbing a mountain near Nagano. The print, he says, is an expression of his temporary blindness, of his reaction to the mountains and to his ordeal. The central area of red surrounded by the black form represents all that he was able to see while afflicted.

30

31

Pl.31f
Umetaro Azechi
Dark Footsteps
1962 $14\frac{1}{2}'' \times 20\frac{1}{4}''$

c

b

e

▲Color separations for Dark Footsteps

a. Block One—1st, 3rd Color
b. Block Two—2nd Color
c. Block Three—4th Color
d. Block Four—5th Color
e. Block Five—6th Color

a

d

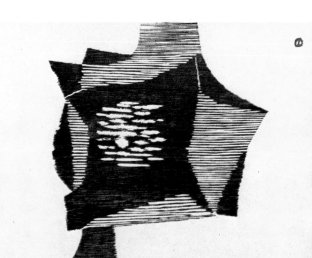

▼Color separations for A Man in Armor

a. Block One—1st Color
b. 1st Color (Reverse side)
c. Block Two—2nd, 7th Color
d. Block Three—3rd Color
e. Block Three—4th, 5th, 8th Color
f. Block Four—6th Color

c

f

b

e

a

d

Pl.32g
Hideo Hagiwara
A Man in Armor
1962   *33½″×23½″*

Hideo Hagiwara

1913   Born, Kofu, Japan.
1929   Returned to Tokyo from Korea where he had spent his early years in a home filled with father's collection of Japanese and Korean art. In Tokyo, studied oil painting with Usaburo Mimino.
1938   Graduated from Tokyo University of Arts. Joined Takamizawa Wood-Cut Company which specialized in making copies of *ukiyo-e*.
1945   Returned to Tokyo after discharge from Army to find his home in ruins.

1953-55 Made first wood block while hospitalized for TB.
1955   Sent one print "Composition L" to International Contemporary Works of Graphic Art from which two hundred copies were made.
1958   Shown in First International Color Print Triannual at Art Society of Grenchen, Switzerland.
1960   Received prize in Second International Print Biennale Tokyo. Shown in Asahi Best Works of 1960, Tokyo. Member of Japan Print Association.
1961   Shown in New Zealand International Print Exhibitions; Modern Japanese Woodcut Exhibition in Italy; and one-man show in Seattle, Washington.
1961-62 Exhibited in North West International Print Exhibition; Cincinnati International Print Biennial; Modern Japanese Woodcut Exhibition, Arts Council of Great Britain, England; Mainichi Contemporary Art Exhibition, Tokyo. Received Grand Prize in Seventh Lugano International Print Exhibition, Switzerland.
1963   Shown in International Art Exhibition of Japan, Tokyo. Received prize "Ljubljana Academy of Arts and Sciences" at print biennial, Yugoslavia. One-man show at Modern Art Museum, Ljubljana; "Gallery 61," Austria; and "Mala Galerija," Yugoslavia.
1964-65 One-man show at Philadelphia Art Alliance and Yoseido Gallery, Tokyo, where he has exhibited since 1956. Lives in Tokyo.

Preparing the Wood-Blocks

The print "Man in Armor"(color plate 32g) is one of a series in which Hagiwara uses the armor of the *Samurai* as his theme. To make this print, he used both sides of two sheets of ⅛ *shina*, three-ply veneer for his four wood-block surfaces. He cut the blocks the same size as the print. In printing, he did not use *kento*, for he had deliberately left no margin on the block, had planned a large print, and had not carved small details or forms that required accurate registry. Instead of the *kento*, he used a strip of paper tacked to the printing table to mark the placement of one corner and one edge of the print paper. And he used a strip of wood, the same thickness as the block, nailed to the table and, one edge of the table itself to register the block.

First Block: (33) Hagiwara uses no preliminary drawing but sketches lines directly on the block with pencil to indicate the basic motif or form. Because he wants the impression from the first block to be printed on the back of the paper, he carves the block in reverse. Hagiwara says that he feels his way intuitively—"forms are suggested, discovered, seen and worked out on the block." Then he uses a large spike to gouge and scribe lines through the first layer of veneer (36). This irregular broken line, so important in the effect of the print, can not be made properly with a knife or chisel.

Hagiwara's approach, while intuitive, suggests much previous thought and experimentation. He knows and predicts technical details. He has the image he wants clearly in mind and he works out the form on the block directly and spontaneously.

Hagiwara removes the first layer of plywood from around his form by making closely spaced, parallel knife cuts (37) and peeling away the wood between these cuts with a flat chisel (38). Then he roughens and bevels the edge of the form left in relief with a nail-studded, wooden *han* (39). He uses a soft wire brush to remove splinters and

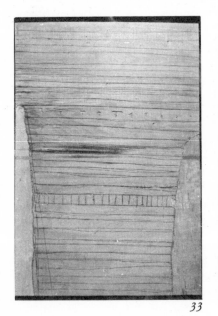

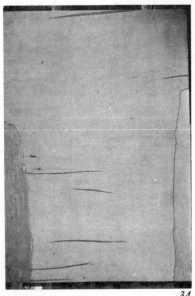

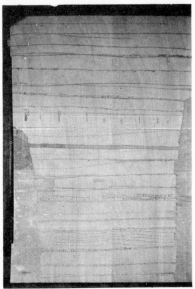

33   34   35

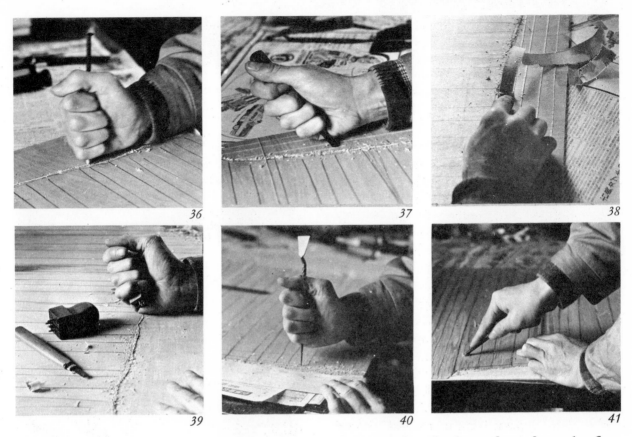

36   37   38

39   40   41

shavings. Now he uses a tinsmith's tool similar to the spike to score further the edges of the form and thus to make it more irregular (40). This roughly beveled line, in contrast to a hard, straight line, added greatly to the plastic effect in the print. He also scribes and gouges lines horizontally across the large form with a V-shaped chisel or veiner, with the spike, and with the tinsmith's tool. He uses the sharp, flat, chisel-like end of the tinsmith's tool to cut away and clean off the splinters created by the scoring. Finally, he uses the spike again to gouge and scribe irregular vertical lines and small holelike shapes across the middle of the block (41).

Second Block: (34) Hagiwara traces and then transfers the large form from the first block onto the back of that block (42). As he has on the first block, he uses the spike to scratch out and scribe the lines. This time he does not soften the edges of the form but leaves them hard. Then he peels away and chisels off the unwanted negative areas on either side of the large form just as he did on the first block.

Third Block: (35) Hagiwara decides to use his third block with the grain running vertically, in contrast to the horizontal grain of the first two blocks. He begins by tracing and then transferring the large form from the first blocks onto block three, the second sheet of veneer. Next he incises two lines with the spike and the tinsmith's tool and pulls the spike across the grain of the wood between the incised lines. This last action will produce the irregular, textured, horizontal bands that show in the finished print (43). Then he removes the negative areas on both sides of the large form as he did on the first and second blocks.

The layers of the *shina* veneer that Hagiwara uses for his blocks are bonded by glue that is more brittle and less binding than that used in marine or waterproofed plywoods. This bonding agent gives the veneer two characteristics significant to the wood-block artist: layers of the block can be easily cut through and peeled away, and the surface of the block splinters and chips in a unique fashion under the pressure of scribing tools. Hagiwara exploits both of these characteristics—the former enables him to work rapidly, the latter enables him to achieve special textural effects in the print (43).

42

Fourth Block: Hagiwara does not carve the fourth block, the back of the third one, for he plans to print from its natural surface a transparent, light green that will cover the entire print (53).

Hagiwara is always making efforts to find new materials, new tools. He seeks constantly to develop new techniques to augment the many traditional *ukiyo-e* methods he now uses. His approach is not haphazard or accidental but the result of study and research. He insists that "One must know, rather than rely on the accidental. Accidents are important, but one must catch, analyze, reconstruct, and utilize things found accidentally. The value lies in the reconstruction and consequent predictability in the printing process. One must never forget that the print must be reproduced and that, therefore, the process must be predictable." And then he

43

44

45

46

47

adds, "It is the small touches—the details with tools, the modeling of the surface of the block—that count."

The Printing Process

Hagiwara says, "The hardest work, and the most physically taxing, is the printing." Before he begins the printing, he prepares his print paper, *hanga torinoko* (Shimizu Seirindo catalog, 16), by leaving dry sheets between wet newspapers until the sheets are thoroughly damp. This dampening process usually requires eight to ten hours, though on rainy or humid days the time may be shorter. The dampened paper allows the pigments and dyes to penetrate deeply into the paper. Using the paper dry will produce an entirely different, more surface effect. The decision to use dry or dampened paper depends upon previous experimentation and on a knowledge of the variety of effects possible. Hagiwara produces the textural effects characteristic of his work by placing the reverse side of his print paper on an already inked block and then using a coarse wire *baren* in such a way that portions of the ink come through to the front or upper surface of the paper. This technique produces the swirl-like textures and mottled patterns evident in the printing of the first block (44, 46).

First Color—Block one: Hagiwara brushes black ink, *bokuju,* on the block several times to saturate it evenly (45). Then he places the *torinoko,* folded lightly in half because of its large size, reverse side down on the block and covers it with a thin, transparent sheet of plastic. Next he rubs the *baren* in a circular motion over the plastic to impress the ink into the paper (46).

The plastic sheet has several uses: It protects the print paper from being torn by the coarse *baren*; it allows the artist to see the degree of penetration, and consequent textured pattern the ink makes as it seeps through to the front of the print; and it keeps the *baren* free of ink that would smudge the print if the *baren* were used directly on the print paper. Notice again that it is the back of the print paper that receives the ink (color plate 32b). Hagiwara creates the surface of his print and the textures he wants on that surface by crushing the fibers of the print paper with the wire *baren* (44), and thus permitting the ink from the block to seep through to the front or surface of the print. He makes a second impression after inking the block one-half at a time to prevent displacement of the paper (45). Because the paper dries quickly, Hagiwara dampens it constantly, especially around the edges, with a wet brush. If the paper dries too quickly, an uneven shrinkage that will alter the registry occurs (color plate 32a, b).

Second Color—Block Two: Hagiwara makes a thin, watery gray from a German dye color, applies it to half the block at a time, and prints (47). He places newspaper over the print paper to keep the *baren* from tearing it (48). The ink in the newspaper acts as a lubricant for the *baren*. For the second printing, he uses a *baren* that contains a wire coil from an electric heater and that is not as coarse as the one used in the first printing. Again, he brushes water along the edges and in the blank spaces of the print to keep it uniformly damp (49). Then he brushes powdered mica evenly over the surface of the print (50). The mica soaks up some of the surface dampness and adds a unique sparkle to the print (color plate 32c).

48

49

50

51

52

53

Third Color—Block Three: Hagiwara uses the same gray dye and the same printing method that he employed for the second printing. He changes the *baren*, however, for one with an even thinner wire core, one that produces a softer, more even effect. He applies his color and prints more than once, as he did in the first printing, to increase the intensity and coverage of the color (color plate 32d).

Fourth Color—Block Three: Taking block three again, which is still damp with the light gray from the third printing, Hagiwara paints the edges of the gouged-out lines and holes in the top half of the block with a thin solution of black dye (51). Because of the dampness of the block and the paper, this technique produces a soft, blurred edge in the print, that has its own special effect. Then he applies the black dye to the area on the block that has produced a dark gray horizontal belt in the print. In orthodox print making, the results that Hagiwara gets through his technique could be obtained only by using a separate block. And he uses the same *baren* and the same printing method that he had used in the third printing (color plate 32d, e).

Fifth Color—Block Three: Again, taking the same block, Hagiwara paints a purple dye in and around the holes and the textured horizontal belt in the bottom half of the block. Then he places the *torinoko* on the block and uses burnisher-like tools to press the paper into the painted areas on the block; the result is the transfer of color from the block to the paper and the creation of an embossed effect in the print (52) (color plate 32e).

At this point, Hagiwara states that he believes that many artists are too engrossed with the immediate surface and do not consider what can be done below the surface of the block.

Sixth Color—Block Four: Hagiwara thinly applies a pale green dye to block four, which is the uncarved, original surface of the reverse side of block three, and prints from it twice (53). He uses the softest of the three *baren* he has thus far employed to impress the color into the print. Then he dusts more mica lightly and evenly over the entire print (54) (color plate 32f).

Seventh Color—Block Two: Returning to his second block, Hagiwara applies a red dye, to which he gives more body by mixing it with red poster paint, to the carved-out areas on each side of the large form (55). Then he places the print paper on the block and uses a large tampon, instead of a *baren,* to press the paper into the block (56). He makes two impressions to intensify the color (color plate 32c).

Eighth Color—Block Three: Taking up his third block, Hagiwara paints with a black dye the carved-out areas on each side of the large form—these areas correspond precisely to those in block two from which he has just printed. He again uses a tampon to impress the color into the paper (56). He twice impresses those portions of the print paper that he had printed in red in the seventh printing. Because the red and black areas on the print, though the same shape, were printed from different blocks, the contrasting textures of the blocks created a more interesting effect than could have been produced by printing the colors from the same block. Then he completes the printing process by brushing another coating of mica powder over the print (color plate 32e, 32g).

Finally, he places the finished print be-tween dry newspapers spread out on a plywood sheet. Then he covers the newspapers with another plywood sheet and weights this sheet.

Hagiwara claims that if the print is allowed to dry in the open, the colors are adversely affected. In addition, the print will, he says, buckle and shrink if it is not dried under pressure. As the prints dry, the color sinks into the paper and becomes lighter. The powdered mica then appears to float on the surface, adding a richness similar to that in the traditional *ukiyo-e* prints on which mica was sometimes applied.

The final effects achieved in the print depend, of course, upon many things. The use of different types of *baren,* for example, produces many different textural and tonal effects. And the degree of wetness of the paper causes the colors to react so as to produce interesting variety. In addition, Hagiwara sometimes uses bleaches to remove areas of the print. Lightening or fading areas in this manner (see "Stone Flower, Red," plate 1) might be called the technique of subtraction to contrast to that of adding new areas with pigment or dye.

54

55

56

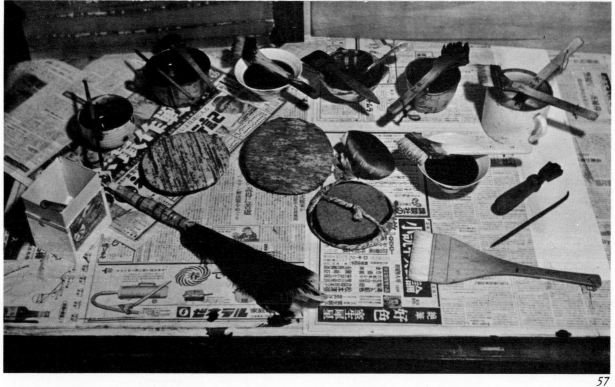

57

73

Sho Kidokoro

1934   Born, Hachioji, Japan. Experience with wood working tools used in family furniture business developed his interest in woodblock printmaking.

1957   Graduated from the Economics Division of Waseda University. Prior interest in art and dislike of future office work decided him on art career.

1958   First exhibited in the annual Hanga Kyokai (Japan Print Association) and with the Modern Art Association. Received prize for print in the Hanga Kyokai exhibit.

1959-61 One-man shows Yoseido Gallery, Tokyo.

1961   Joined the Hanga Kyokai. Exhibited in the American Color Print Association Show in Philadelphia and in the Philippine Art Association Exhibit in Manila.

1962   Became a member of the Modern Art Association, Tokyo. Exhibited in the Painters' and Sculptors' Association Show in Israel. Work shown in the Traveling Print Exhibition in Australia.

1963-65 Exhibited in the annual Hanga Kyokai print exhibitions, and in many group shows both in Japan and abroad. Lives in Hachioji, Japan.

59

60

The "One-Block" Process

The print "Broken Flag" (color plate 33f), like many of Kidokoro's prints, is unusual in that it was printed from a single block, in contrast to the several blocks ordinarily used for color printing. Kidokoro creates his single-block color prints by alternately working on the block and the printing until he is satisfied with the result. He says, "The point at which I feel I should stop is reached when nothing more can be done or said." (Because the results of this method are less predictable than those produced by the usual methods, one must work more intuitively, take advantage of accidental happenings during the preparation of the block, and have a thorough knowledge of what the material can do.) Kidokoro does not make a definite or detailed drawing preparatory to carving the block. He uses preliminary sketches only to define the initial image, which is then modified during the carving and printing stages (59). He feels that his most successful works are produced in a "flash sort of manner"—a spontaneous, almost automatic way—that is most suitable for the one-block method. The technical explanations that follow cannot, therefore, be presented as before, with a description of the preparation of the block followed by one of the printing methods used, but must alternate between the carving and the printing techniques employed. Usually Kidokoro prints about ten editions of a print made by the one-block method. He cannot, of course, make reprints of the finished work because he alters the surface of the block permanently at almost every stage in the development of the print.

First Stage: (60) After he sketches the image on a block of ½-inch *shina* veneer, Kidokoro

61

62

63

64

applies white vinyl wall paint to the block with a spatula to build various forms in relief. He uses an electric drill to scribe lines and textured areas over the block (61). And he employs traditional Japanese wood-block tools to carve out additional lines and forms and to make the *kento* for registering the print paper (62). Kidokoro uses the drill like a drawing tool, with quick, light strokes that produce a unique line quality that cannot be made with any other tool. Because the drill raises a burrlike edge, the artist smooths and cleans the surface for printing with sandpaper and a soft wire brush.

Before printing, Kidokoro moistens several large sheets of sized *kizuki-hosho* (Yamada Shokai catalog, 42) with a large *shoji* brush. He then places the sheets on top

of one another to soak for about fifteen minutes before using. He dampens the block thoroughly and wipes off excess water with a dry rag. Then he thins a liquid black carbon ink (*bokuju*) with water and brushes the resulting brownish-gray color over the entire block (63). Now he places a sheet of the dampened *kizuki-hosho* on the block and registers it with the *kento*. He puts a sheet of wrapping paper over the print to protect it from the coarse *baren*, which he then rubs over the wrapping paper with a back-and-forth motion across the width of the print (64). (This *baren* was made from a coil of twisted wire held together by a round piece of paper that is glued to one side of the coil, topped with a round piece of thin plywood the same diameter as the coil, and wrapped with the traditional bamboo husk covering.) Kidokoro prints each sheet twice to build up the tone and depth of the color (65). He makes five sheets or runs before he begins the second stage (color plate 33a).

Second Stage: Kidokoro does not alter the block for the second printing. He develops the print in the second stage by applying color to the three distinct areas on the block (66). He begins by brushing *nori*, a paste, over the top area of the block. Then he brushes Holbein's viridian watercolor over the form in this area and prints with a *baren* that contains a sandpaper "coil." (The sandpaper *baren* produces a finer, more even impression than the coarser wire *baren*, and Kidokoro used it for all the printing in the second stage.) After printing the top area, Kidokoro folds the paper back to expose the middle area. He then paints this area with *nori* and brushes a mixture of black carbon ink and black poster paint over

it and prints again. Finally, he folds back the print again and prepares the third area by painting over it with the rice paste and applying a dull red, made by mixing carmine watercolor with a light red poster paint. As in the first stage, Kidokoro prints five sheets and then washes the block for the next step (color plate 33b). (In all of the printings in the second stage, Kidokoro used color sparingly. He made additional applications of color and took repeated impressions to build up a more opaque quality. He seldom expects the first impression to be final. He uses *nori* because it causes the color to adhere more effectively to the paper. But *nikawa*, a glue made from ox or horse hooves, can also be used. Because the day was sunny and the air dry, Kidokoro repeatedly sprayed the block with water from an atomizer to keep the *nori* and paint moist (67). This is especially important when using the *nori*, for it will cause the paper to stick to the block

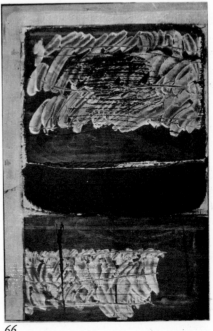

65   66

67

68

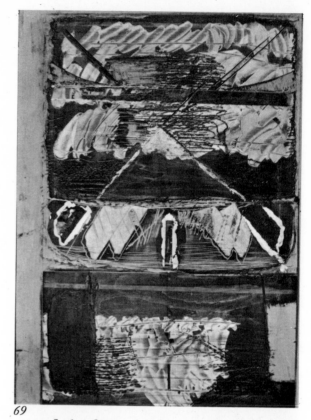

69

if it becomes too dry.)

Third stage: (69) Kidororo first sketches in pencil on the black middle area of the block. He tears and cuts to size the pieces of paper —small scraps of *torinoko*—and pastes them on the black area over the line previously sketched in pencil (68). He pastes a longer strip of paper on the top area of the block. Using a spatula, he then applies white vinyl paint over and around the paper forms (68). When the paint sets, Kidokoro removes several of the paper shapes (70). (This action produces a different type of relief surface because of the straight edges and depressed or negative areas left in the shapes made by the vinyl paint.) Then he uses the edge of the spatula to add more relief lines (72). And he again uses the electric drill to scribe lines

around the forms made with the paper and vinyl paint (71). Now he waterproofs with lacquer the paper shapes that remain glued to the block to protect them during the printing process. And he uses a wood-block chisel or gouge to carve out unwanted areas and to deepen some of the lines scribed in the block with the drill (73). Then he sands the block to remove the burrlike edges in preparation for the printing.

As in the second stage, Kidokoro uses different colors for the top, middle and bottom areas of his block. And he applies *nori* first, as before. He uses straight black carbon ink for the top area, white poster paint grayed slightly by the addition of black carbon ink for the middle area, and a mixture of the black ink and carmine watercolor for

70

71

72

73

74

75

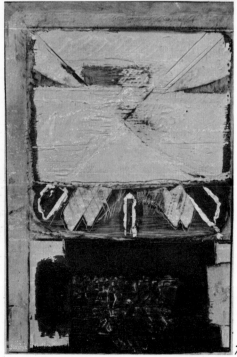

76

the bottom area. Kidokoro makes several impressions before he feels satisfied with the quality of the color. He uses the soft *baren*, containing the sandpaper, to print the top and middle areas, and the wire *baren* to print the bottom one. Because the print paper becomes increasingly damp from repeated printings, Kidokoro uses wrapping paper to protect the print and to provide a smoother surface for the *baren* to slide over. After he prints five editions or sheets, he washes the block thoroughly to remove the accumulated pigments (color plate 33c).

Fourth Stage: Kidokoro begins by chiseling out portions of the top and bottom areas of his block (75) and lightly sanding the rough edges left by the chiseling. Then he brushes white poster paint, grayed with the ink, over the top area of the block (74) and prints from it lightly with the soft, or sandpaper *baren*. Next he brushes black ink on the bottom area and prints from it with the soft *baren*. As in the second and third stages, Kidokoro uses *nori* and keeps the block moist by spraying it with water. As before, he prints five runs and then cleans the block with water (color plate 33d).

Fifth and Last Stage: (76)Kidokoro decides upon a fifth step after several days pass because he had originally considered the print finished at the completion of the fourth stage. He makes changes by carving out portions of the bottom area and then printing from the new forms thus made with the same color used in the fourth stage. He uses the same soft *baren* and the same printing techniques to complete the editions (color plate 33f).

Pl.33. Sho Kidokoro *Broken Flag* 1963 21½″×33¼″

a

b

c

d

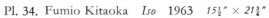

Pl. 34. Fumio Kitaoka   *Iso*   1963 $15\frac{1}{2}'' \times 21\frac{3}{4}''$

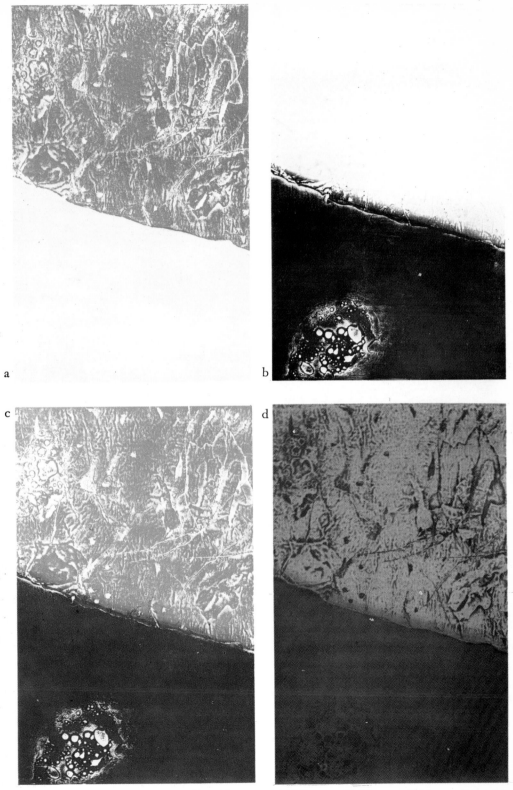

a

b

c

d

Pl. 35. Hiroyuki Tajima   *Tajidemo*   1963 $12\frac{1}{2}'' \times 16\frac{3}{4}''$

Pl.36. Hodaka Yoshida *Tsuzumi* 1962 *16" × 22"*

Pl. 36

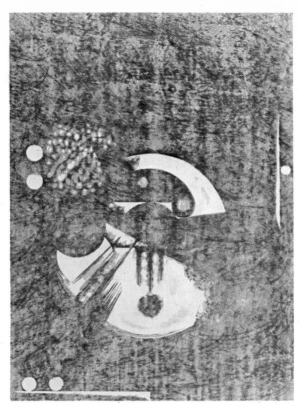

a. 1st Printing • Block 1

b. 2nd Printing • Block 2

c. 3rd Printing • Block 2

d. 4th Printing • Block 3

e. 5th Printing • Block 4

f. 6th Printing • Block 5

g. 7th Printing • Block 6

h. 8th Printing • Block 4

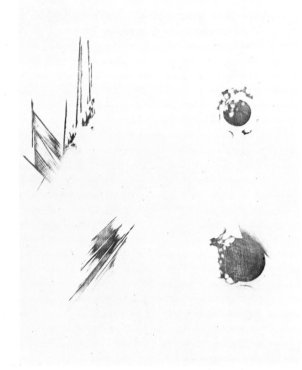

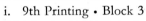

i. 9th Printing • Block 3

j. 10th Printing • Block 5

k. 11th Printing • Block 6

l. 12th Printing • Block 7

Pl. 36

m. 13th Printing • Block 8

n. 14th Printing • Block 7

o. 15th Printing • Block 4

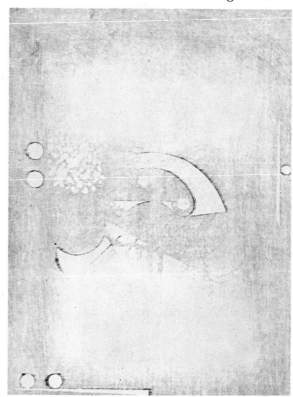

p. 16th Printing • Block 1

Hiroyuki Tajima

1911   Born, Tokyo, Japan.

1932   Graduated from the Art Department of Nippon University. Graduated from the Tokyo School of Art (Ueno). Learned fabric dyeing techniques from Matsugoro Hirokawa. After leaving the art school, he studied watercolor painting with Toshio Nakanishi.

1941–45   Served in an army construction unit.

1946   Met Yoshishige Saito and began painting abstract oils under his tutelage. Joined and exhibited with the Bijutsu Bunka Kyokai, a group instrumental in bringing back the abstract-surrealist movement suppressed during the war. Produced first wood-block prints. Instructed by the veteran printmaker Yoshiro Nagase.

1949–54   Experimented with color-photo processing and printing techniques at the Yamatoya photo printing company. Results of experience later used to augment his wood-block printing techniques.

1950–56   Stopped painting to write short stories and poetry, and to study the art of tea ceremony and flower arrangement.

1962   Exhibited in the Northwest International Prints Exhibition at Seattle, Washington, and the 5th Contemporary Art Exhibition of Japan sponsored by the Mainichi Newspapers, Tokyo.

1963–65   Member of the Japan Print Association. One-man show at Yoseido Gallery, Tokyo. Prints are in numerous collections all over the world. Lives in Yokohama, Japan.

Preparing the Block

The print (color plate 35d) Tajima created to demonstrate his technique is essentially the product of an additive rather than a cutting away or subtractive process. Characteristically, Tajima prepares his wood blocks for printing by applying paper, shellac, and lacquer to the block to build up the image in relief, and by cutting or scratching linear forms into the relief surface of the block.

Prior to making the block, Tajima prepares the following materials: He paints one side of *gampi* or tracing paper evenly with shellac—usually he prepares a month's supply of this paper at one time; he cuts two sheets of veneer, one of ⅛ inch *rawan* veneer and one of ⅛ inch *shina* veneer, the same size as the print; and then he makes a quantity of shellac. (He makes the shellac by first filling a pint jar with dried shellac flakes, then adding menthyl alcohol until it is absorbed by the dry shellac, and then filling the jar with the alcohol. He allows the mixture to stand until the shellac is thoroughly dissolved.)

First Block: Tajima pencils the design directly on the block. Then he stains the *shina* block with a light wash of *bokuju* (carbon ink) so that the lines to be incised can be seen clearly. He says that the first sketchy lines represent the image as it was in his mind. Then he intuitively elaborates upon this first sketch, relating lines and mass as he progresses. Tajima feels that his near-spontaneous approach is similar to that of the "action" painter, except that he must constantly be aware of the effects the preparation will create in the finished print.

Now Tajima cuts a large piece of shellac paper the same shape as the form penciled on the block (78). He paints the back of the paper and the entire surface of the block with shellac and presses the shaped paper on the block (79). Then, he applies more shellac to fix in place the loose edges. Next, he uses a woodcutting knife and chisel to cut textured areas on the block and to cut and rearrange areas of the shellac paper affixed to the block (80). Again he applies shellac to seal and glue down the loose edges (81).

Then Tajima paints the back of pieces of torn shellac paper and glues them to the

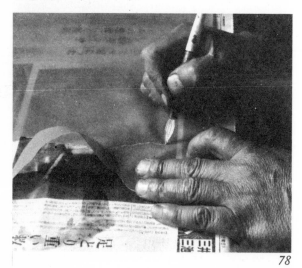

78

79

block to build up the forms he wants. He uses an awl-like tool to scribe lines through the paper and into the block, following the lines of the initial sketch, and applies more shellac over the block. Again, he glues more small pieces of shellac paper to the block to build up the relief surface. Then he allows the shellac to dry before he continues.

Next, he cuts and trims the excess shellac paper from the edges of the block. He uses the awl-like tool and a V-shaped chisel or veiner to enlarge and deepen the lines that he has already scratched or cut into the block. Then, by rotating a U-shaped chisel or gouge, he makes several small holes (82). Note: All the above applies to the upper half of the block, the half on which Tajima has applied shellac paper.

Tajima now brushes white lacquer on the block to make two circular forms. After each form is made, he drops from a *sumi-e* brush several large drops of water on the surface of the lacquer and then splatters the lacquer forms with water from his fingertips (83). (The water droplets sink through the lacquer and displace it, producing crater-like forms of various sizes.) After the lacquer

81

82

80

83

dries, Tajima carefully removes the water with an absorbent rag. He completes the first block by using a flat chisel to soften the ridges that appear on the edges of the lacquered forms at the top of the block (84, 85).

Second Block: Tajima does not carve or treat in any way the surface of the second block, the *rawan* veneer, because he plans to use it as it is (90).

The application of materials of all kinds to the surface of the block—string, sawdust, sand, paper, glue, plaster, enamel, lacquer and plastics, there is no end to the materials that can be used—with which to build a relief surface, is a technique that has been employed in various ways for many years, but its creative potential is far from exhausted.

84

The Printing Process

In addition to the conventional printing techniques, Tajima utilizes a resist process, the results of which characterize his prints. School children use a similar resist technique when they draw on paper with wax crayons and paint over the drawing with black poster paint. The wax crayon drawing on the paper resists the paint—only the paper absorbs the paint—and the areas colored by the crayons remain unchanged. Because the colors are isolated in a dark field, and because the white ground (here the white paper) under the areas colored by the crayons is not altered by the paint, the colors glow and remain pure. Tajima's method is based on the same principle. He first prints fine artist's colors on the paper and then prints (more often brushes) a fabric dye (usually the darkest color) over the entire print surface. The oil colors resist the dye. Only the exposed or unprinted areas of the paper absorb the dye color. It is important to understand the advantage this method offers over the usual one of printing the same colors over a dark surface. The resist method allows the paper under the areas printed with oil colors to remain white. This whiteness reflects light through the oil colors and thereby adds a richness and depth one cannot obtain by printing the same colors on a dark field.

First Color—Block One: Tajima squeezes out artists' colors—zinc white, Prussian blue, and blue compose—on a sheet of plate glass. He adds several drops of medium (a mixture of 40 percent linseed oil and 60 percent turpentine) and uses a palette knife to mix them into the colors. A small amount of medium must be added to make the oil paint resist the dye color more effectively, as well as to improve the printing qualities of the paint. Then he takes a medium-hard roller and rolls the paint over the glass until both glass and roller are evenly coated (86).

In color printing, it is important that one not overload the roller with pigment, as this will generally produce prints with an unpleasant, cheap surface quality.

Tajima rolls the first color onto the upper part of the block, to which he has applied the shellac paper; then he carefully wipes off any paint that has been rolled past the edges of the form (87). Next, he places the block in a wooden registry frame tacked parallel to the edge of the table (88). For the frame, Tajima carefully selects strips of wood that are slightly less thick than the block so as not to obstruct the printing process. Tajima registers the paper, *torinoko* (Shimizu Seirindo catalog, 16), used dry, by thumbtacking it on the corner of the table

85

86

87

88

and using the edges of the table as a guide (88). Tajima, like Hagiwara, does not carve the traditional *kento* into his blocks. He then places the print paper over the block and "irons" with the *baren*, first moving the *baren* lengthwise to the paper, then moving it crosswise, and finally moving it with circular strokes (89). This completes the first printing (color plate 35a). Tajima then thoroughly cleans the block with turpentine, which he must do after each printing or the oil paint will build up and clog the surface of the block. Because he has painted the block with shellac, which is impervious to oil paint, he is able to clean the surface easily.

Second Color—Block One: Tajima prepares the second color, a mixture of Prussian blue and a small amount of zinc white, and rolls the dark blue color on the bottom half of the block with a soft roller. He uses a one-inch brush, which he has dipped in turpentine, to soften and graduate the edge of the dark blue color area where it merges with the bottom edge of the upper form that has been printed with the first color. Then he again places the block in the registry frame and takes the impression (color plate 35b, c).

Third Color—Block Two: It is his use of the third color, a dye color, which makes Tajima's prints unique. He prepares a CIBA textile dye, coprantine blue G-11 300%, by mixing a teaspoonful of the dye with one cup of water and boiling the mixture for six or seven minutes. While the dye is boiling, he adds a pinch of salt, which acts to set the dye color after it is applied to the print.

Tajima then brushes water over the surface of the *rawan* block until the block is

89

90

evenly saturated. He places about a cup of the blue dye in a shallow bowl and adds about six drops of *rodo* oil to the dye. Then he brushes this mixture on the second block and makes the impression (90). Because the dye color penetrates and softens the paper, Tajima places a newspaper over the print before he takes the impression with the *baren;* without this protection, the print would be torn by the action of the *baren.*

It is necessary for Tajima to make two applications of the dye-color before the paper absorbs the dye completely; this completes the printing process (color plates 35d). Tajima then rolls out a sample of each color he has used and places the sample in the notebook that he keeps for recording the edition, colors, title and date of each print that he makes.

The *rodo* oil, a type of castor oil emulsion that mixes with water, acts much like a wetting agent. Tajima adds one teaspoon of

91

the *rodo* oil to one pint of water and brushes the solution over the areas of the print that he is going to dye. After the *rodo* oil solution has dried, he brushes on the straight dye color and makes the impression. He uses the *rodo* oil and water solution because paper that is treated with this solution absorbs the dye color more readily and evenly than does paper that is not so treated. To save time, Tajima applies the *rodo* oil and dye color mixture together when he makes the demonstration print; this method can be used for smaller prints, without making any discernible difference in the finished print. The dye and *rodo* oil mixture can also be brushed on the prints (91); this is sometimes a quicker and more easily controllable method when used with small prints. Larger prints, because of their greater area, should first be treated with *rodo* oil and water solution and be allowed to dry before the dye color is brushed or printed on and the impression is made. Commercial wetting agents can be substituted for the *rodo* oil, just as various brands of textile (cotton) dye may be used in place of the CIBA dye that Tajima uses.

Because the dye color will slightly darken or tint the oil color when the dye color is printed over the oil color, the oil color used should be a shade or two lighter than that desired in the finished print; how much lighter the oil color should be varies with the dye used and is determined only by experience. Tajima occasionally applies various dye colors to different parts of the print, and in this process the dye can be printed or brushed on in the same way as has been described. Because thinner solutions of dye color are transparent, dye colors can also be printed over each other to create new color combinations.

Fumio Kitaoka

1918   Born, Tokyo, Japan.

1940   First exhibited woodblock prints at Japan Print Association (Hanga Kyokai) Tokyo. Studied with Un'ichi Hiratsuka.

1941-42 Graduated from Tokyo University of Arts. Oils exhibited in the Shunyo-kai exhibit, Tokyo. Member of the Japan Print Association. Taught art at the Gyosei school, Tokyo.

1945   Traveled to Manchuria.

1953   Print shown in the International Art Exhibition, Tokyo, and each year after. Work exhibited in the International Biennale, São Paulo.

1955   Traveled to France where he studied wood engraving at the École Nationale des Beaux-Arts. Prints shown at Salon de Réalité Nouvelle.

1956   Visited Italy on return to Japan. Prints shown in the International Exhibition of Graphic Art, Lugano, Switzerland.

1957   Prints shown in the Biennale, São Paulo; International Graphic Arts show, Ljubljana; Sosaku Hanga Exhibition, Art Institute of Chicago; and the Northwest Printmakers 32nd International Exhibit, Seattle.

1962-65 Has had numerous one-man shows and exhibited in many group shows abroad. Traveled to the United States, 1964–65, to teach wood-block printing at the Minneapolis Museum School of Art. Lives in Tokyo.

Preparing the Blocks

Kitaoka's most recent work reflects his interest in nature, especially in the power and solitude of the sea and its shores. The print (color plate 34d) made for the demonstration is an expression of the sea's effect—as the tide recedes and deposits its varied life—on rocks that had been recently submerged. Kitaoka took the idea for the print from one of the many sketches he had made at the seashore (93) and then worked it out in greater detail on a larger sheet of paper. He used black Conté crayon for the drawing and added details by painting over the drawing with watercolors (94). He transferred the drawing to the block by placing it face down on the block, and then rubbing the back with a *baren* to impress the heavy black Conté lines onto the block (96). He then drew over the lines on the block to delineate more clearly the forms and to alter and add to the initial image. He carved five blocks—these blocks were $\frac{1}{4}$ inch *shina* veneer with a thick *rawan* center ply and were cut slightly larger than the print so that *kento* could be carved on the margins. But after printing from all five, he decided to use only the three that are described here. He made frequent changes as he worked; several of the forms carved on the second block do not appear in the finished print.

Block One: (101) The block Kitaoka carves first, which is also the key block, is one he plans to use second in the printing process. He carves lines and small forms in this block

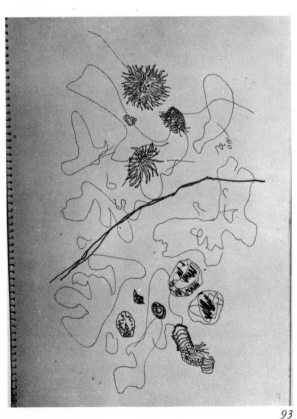

93

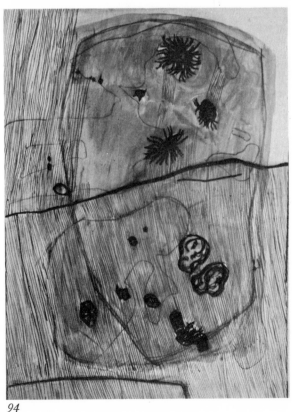

94

with a small V-shaped veiner, a small U-shaped chisel, and a Japanese wood-block knife (95). During the carving, Kitaoka rubs black Conté over the surface of the block to make it contrast with the carved-out areas and to give a more accurate impression of how the block will look when printed. Then he chisels out an area on the top and right side, leaving a thin margin on the outer edge for the *kento* (97). Finally, he uses a knife and a ruler to trim the edges of the printing surface of the block.

96

95

97

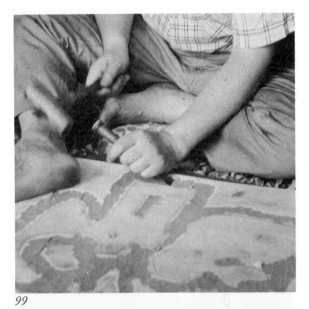

98 99

100

Block Two: (102) Kitaoka traces the drawing onto the block, as before, and uses a small U-shaped chisel to cut around the small forms. Then he uses a gouge to carve out an area around the small forms so as to isolate and place them in higher relief for the printing. Next, he carves the small details inside the forms with the small gouge, the veiner, and the Japanese knife (98). He plans to print block two last in the printing sequence.

Block Three: (103) Kitaoka traces an image onto the third block, which he will use first in printing, and then carves it as he has block two. After he carves around the forms with the small U-shaped gouge (99), he gouges away about two inches of the surrounding negative area, using a larger gouge. He does not bother to carve away all the unwanted areas of the block because he feels such carving is both unnecessary and time-consuming. Leaving negative areas level with the forms to be printed serves to support the print during the printing and prevents it from stretching and sagging into the cutout areas. Next, he bevels slightly, with a flat chisel, the edges of the large,

amoeba-like forms to soften and eliminate the hard edge that would otherwise appear in the print. Because the glue in the plywood was strong, Kitaoka could not peel away layers of the veneer, but had to chisel away the wood as if the block were solid.

Note: Kitaoka later carved additional forms in block three to modify the initial print. These changes can be seen if the photograph of the block is contrasted to the photograph of the first printing.

Kitaoka seldom carves the blocks in the order in which he prints from them. Usually, he carves first the most important or key block and then the blocks containing the color areas. He makes test prints and then necessary changes in the blocks—or recarves the block completely—until he obtains the results he wants.

The Printing Process

First Kitaoka dampens the printing paper, *torinoko* (Yamada Shokai catalogue, 28), with a large *shoji* brush, places it between damp sheets of newspaper, and covers the

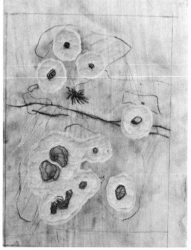

101   *102*   *103*

100

104

105

106

newspaper with plywood boards. He leaves the paper to soak for about ten minutes while he prepares for printing.

He begins these preparations by dampening small pads of newspaper and placing them under the workboard to keep it from slipping. Then he puts a wet cloth over the workboard to keep the wood blocks from slipping and to keep them moist. He brushes both sides of the blocks with water (104) and places the blocks on the wet cloth covering the workboard. Before he prints from each block, he mixes in small saucers the colors to be used (107).

First Printing—Block Three: Kitaoka mixes Guitar brand, ivory black, and white poster paint, thins the resulting warm gray mixture with water, and then brushes it evenly over the dampened block (105). Next, he registers the dampened paper on the block and rubs with the *baren* lightly but constantly for over a minute to ensure an even impression (106) (color plate 34a). Finally, he uses a newspaper to blot excess color from the print.

107

Ordinarily, wood-block printers apply camellia oil to the *baren* to make it slide easily over the back of the print, but Kitaoka used hair cream, which is just as effective.

The mottled effect in the print was produced by a slight unevenness in the surface of the block. This effect is precisely what Kitaoka wanted. He could not, however, predict it absolutely, for there is always a slight degree of uncertainty in the printing.

Second Printing—Block One: Kitaoka mixes equal parts of *bokuju* (black carbon ink) and black poster paint, and then brushes the mixture over the dampened block (108). Because of the intricate lines he has carved into the block, he is careful not to use too much paint, for it can easily clog the space between the lines and so blur the print. He registers the print paper (109), places a sheet of paper over the print, and applies the *baren* lightly. He then brushes the black paint over the block a second time and prints again to deepen the color and to ensure that all the forms and lines have been solidly printed (color plate 22b).

Third Printing—Block Two: Kitaoka uses four colors for the last printing. He mixes *Shiseido* watercolors and white poster paint in the following combinations: chrome yellow and sky blue for the large orange forms; chrome yellow for the top right form; and viridian and chrome green for the remaining shapes. He brushes the colors on the block with oil painter's flat bristle brushes (111). Then he places the print on the block and rubs the *baren* lightly over the back of the print to take the impression (color plate 34c, 34d). His final step is to place the print between newspapers and cover the newspapers with a sheet of ply-

108

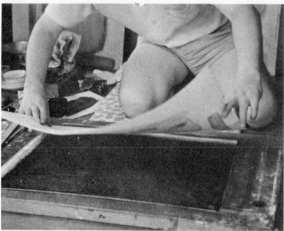

109

110

111

112

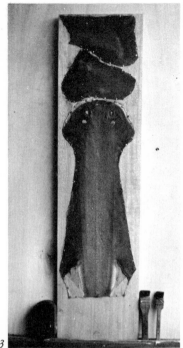

113

wood. He leaves the print under pressure to dry slowly for a day.

Kitaoka insists that the print paper must be evenly damp during all stages of the printing for best results. Usually the margins of the print dry first and need dampening occasionally to maintain an even moisture.

To prepare the traditional brushes used in applying the paint to the block—and this is usually done before using a new brush of this type—the artist begins by singeing the end hairs or bristles with a match. Then he holds the brush perpendicular to the surface of a dried sharkskin, which he has tacked to a board, and rubs the brush against the grain or tooth of the skin. The sharp, rough sharkskin splits and frays the ends of the hairs in the brush and so produces a finer, more softly tipped brush that can be used effectively to brush paint on the blocks (112), (113).

Hodaka Yoshida

1926   Born, Tokyo, Japan. Father was noted wood-block artist; however, he desired Hodaka to pursue other interests.

1949   Graduated from the Science Department of Daiichi Higher School (now Tokyo University). While a student, wrote and published poetry (*waka*) and developed interest in painting.

1950   Began making first wood-block prints.

1952   Exhibited oils and wood-block prints at Maruzen, Tokyo.

1953   Member of Japan Print Association (Hanga Kyokai). Traveled to the United States, Cuba and Mexico. The ancient pre-Spanish art of Mexico left a deep impression and greatly influenced his later work.

1957   Traveled to the United States to teach Japanese wood-block techniques at the University of Hawaii, University of Oregon and Haystack Mountain School of Crafts. Returned to Japan via Europe and Asia. One-man shows in Tokyo and Landau Gallery, Los Angeles.

1958-65   Exhibited in the Biennale de Paris, Biennale of Prints, Tokyo, and in numerous shows in Tokyo and abroad. Received prize at the 7th International Exhibition at Lugano, Switzerland, 1962. Has written extensively on wood-block printing in various publications. Traveled to the United States, 1963, to represent Japan at the International Print Conference held in New York City. Lives in Tokyo.

Preparing the Blocks

Hodaka Yoshida is a technical master. His skills at once represent and exalt the high craft standards that hold in the Japanese print movement. But his superb craftsmanship does not in any way diminish his creativity. He combines traditional Japanese printing methods—derived in part from *ukiyo-e* techniques—with his own innovations to create powerful, rhythmic abstractions that are very different from the traditional Japanese print. Yoshida feels that the technique is only the means—the *han*, or block, of *hanga*—through which to achieve the art, or *ga*. "It is the art that must be emphasized," he says. "Oil painters must also try wood block," he adds, "for artists working in other media will see the woodblock medium in new ways and introduce new ideas."

When asked how he begins his work, Yoshida points to a sketchbook filled with small abstractions sketched in pencil (115). From these sketches he develops the images for the demonstration print (117). Using the sketches as a guide, he develops the drawing on a sheet of paper the same size as the block. He draws in a very precise manner, using a compass and ruler to delineate the forms and lines (116). As the drawing progresses, he draws certain forms and lines in colored pencil in order to relate them to the specific blocks on which they will later

115

116

117

105

be traced and carved. Although the original drawing is quite precise, Yoshida uses it only as a guide, for he feels that if he follows the drawing too closely the final print will be stiff and forced.

After he has completed the drawing, Yoshida cuts to size eight sheets of five-ply, *shina* veneer, about $\frac{3}{8}$ inches thick. He uses this plywood, originally made for the production of ping-pong rackets, because the

glue binding the plywood is weak, and he can therefore more easily cut and peel the layers of wood from the block during the carving process than he could if the glue were strong.

After he cuts the blocks to size, Yoshida brushes a thin gray wash of *sumi* ink over the blocks before tracing the forms (118). He does this to obtain added contrast between the cutout areas and the forms which emerge

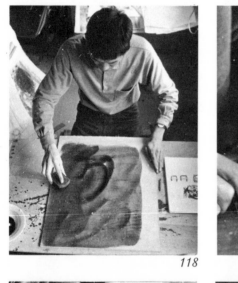

118

119

120

121

122

123

during the carving process.

Since Yoshida used essentially the same carving methods to prepare all the eight blocks used in the print —as can be seen in the photographs of the eight blocks—it is unnecessary to describe in detail the carving of each block; therefore, a description of the carving of only one block—block two in the series—is given.

After placing the drawing face up over sheets of red carbon paper (116), Yoshida traces the drawing onto the block; he then makes minor changes on the block, changes which he feels are necessary to correct and add to the original forms and lines. Next, he uses a Japanese wood-block knife to cut, at a slight angle away from the edge, around the large form; then he chisels and peels away the unwanted or negative areas (119). Because he removes only the first layer initially, he makes a second cutting and removes the second layer of veneer in order to deepen the negative spaces and to place the remaining form in higher relief for the printing. Then he cleans and smooths the cutout areas with a flat chisel. Next, Yoshida uses a veiner and ⌐-shaped chisel to cut out the linear areas (120). Because the lines are thin, he makes certain that the cuts are beveled away from the lines so that they will not be undercut or weakened. He then uses a shallow gouge to chisel out very shallow, round depressions in the upper right area of the block; and he uses sandpaper to soften the round, mottled-appearing forms made with the gouge (121). Yoshida also carves these shallow areas, used to give texture to the finished print, on the first block. He uses a smaller, less shallow U-shaped gouge to carve out similar but more distinct, rounded, cellular-like forms on blocks 3,5,6 and 7.

Yoshida then lightly sands the edges of the larger form in order to eliminate the hard edge effect that will otherwise be produced in the print. To produce an even softer edge in the print, he slightly bevels the forms with a flat chisel and sandpaper.

This method can also be used to achieve a graduated tone in the print, because more or less color will be impressed into the paper in direct proportion to the degree of bevel

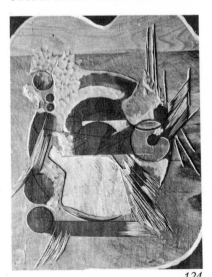

124

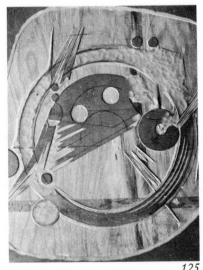

125

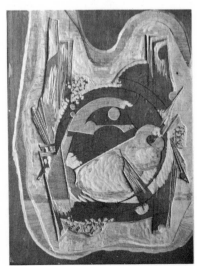

126

or taper which is made in the form carved on the block.

Yoshida's technique for carving the blocks can be summarized as follows. He traces the drawing onto the block and then, with the Japanese knife, he cuts the forms. Next, using a flat chisel, he chisels and peels off the negative or unwanted areas. He carves intricate lines with a V-shaped veiner and ⌐-shaped chisel, and he carves or scoops out the mottled, cellular-like textured areas with a U-shaped gouge. Last, he carves the *kento* in each block to register the prints (130). It takes him approximately 15 hours to carve the blocks.

"Carving the block," Yoshida says, "is like painting without color—using tools in place of loaded brushes" (131).

The Printing Process

The carving of the blocks requires the most time and physical effort of the artist; the printing of the blocks requires the most skill. If the artist is to produce a predictable result in each phase or step of the printing —sometimes, of course, he is able to make use of accidental happenings—the artist must know what the materials can do. The effects produced by the amount and kind of color used, by the degree of dampness of the paper and the type of paper used, by the surface characteristics of the block, must all be known and predictable. The artist can acquire this knowledge and skill only through experience.

First Printing—Block One: Yoshida uses a thick, sized *kizuki-hosho* paper (Yamada Shokai catalog, 42) that he first dampens by brushing water over the back of the paper with a wide *shoji* brush a few minutes before he starts the printing (132). He also dampens the block so that the paint will not be soaked up by the dry wood. If a dry block is used in the printing, the results of the impression are not predictable, as the colors will sink into the block in some areas and will remain moist in others. Therefore, the wood-block artists first dampen with water all the blocks to be used in the printing process before they brush on the paint.

Yoshida next brushes the block with the

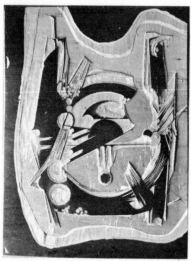

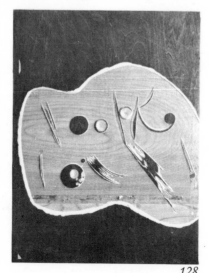

127

128

129

color, Holbein's yellow ochre watercolor, mixed with black *sumi* ink (*Kaime* carbon ink), and thinned with water; he brushes on the color with a circular motion until the surface of the block is evenly saturated. Then he lines up the *kizuki-hosho* paper in the *kento*, for registry, and places the paper on the block. He uses a four-strand *baren* to make the impression, rubbing it across the back of the paper with a moderate pressure; he varies the pressure on the *baren* to produce slight tonal variations in the print (134). He uses the four-strand *baren* only for the first printing; for the rest of the printing, he uses an eight-strand *baren* that has a finer, less rough bamboo fiber coil inside.

Next, Yoshida removes the print from the block and places newspapers on the face of the print to absorb the excess paint. He blots up, with a damp sheet of newspaper, any areas of the white paper that are smudged with the gray color. Then he allows the print to dry for about five minutes before continuing with the second printing. (See color plates 36f, g, h and i for first and additional printings.)

130

131

132

133

Second Printing—Block Two: Yoshida mixes Holbein's cobalt blue watercolor and black *sumi* ink, thins with water, and brushes the mixture lightly on the block (133). He uses the eight-strand or standard *baren*, with moderate pressure, to make the impression. This time, he prints twice in order to deepen the color.

Third Printing—Block Two: Using *sumi* ink diluted with water, Yoshida brushes color on a circular area that has been drawn, but not cut, in the center of the block. He then places the print in position on the block and places a thin *hosho* paper—actually two sheets of paper with sand glued between them—over the print. He rubs the *hosho* paper with a small, flat piece of wood, instead of with the *baren*, because the covering of the *baren* would be torn if it were rubbed over the gritty surface of the sand-impregnated paper.

Fourth Printing—Block Three: First, Yoshida lightly brushes water over the face of the print. Then, he mixes Talen's purple —all the Talen paints used in the print are designers' colors made in Holland—and Holbein's cobalt blue watercolor, thins the mixture with water, and brushes the resultant color lightly over the block. After he has applied the *baren* and made the impression, he blots the print with newspaper.

Yoshida uses the first colors very thinly; he adds more opaque colors as the print nears completion. While the paper is damp and the colors are used thinly, the colors sink into the paper and merge with the other colors. The more opaque colors remain on the surface of the print and produce a contrast that adds much depth to the finished print.

Fifth Printing—Block Four: Yoshida dampens the print again and applies Holbein's ultramarine blue watercolor from the tube directly onto the wet block, brushing the color out evenly on the block. Then he makes the impression. Because the paper, at this stage of the process, is quite damp, he places a newspaper over the print before

134

135

using the *baren*. He does this to protect the print from tearing, and also to make it easier to use the *baren*, for the ink in the newspaper acts as a lubricant. He then again blots the print with newspaper.

Sixth Printing—Block Five: First, Yoshida lightly brushes water over the face of the print (136) and the surface of the block. He then mixes together equal amounts of Holbein's burnt umber and sepia watercolor, thins the mixture with water, and brushes the color on the block. Placing newspaper over the print, which has been registered on the block, he uses the *baren* lightly to impress the color into the print. He again blots the print with newspaper to remove excess moisture and paint.

Seventh Printing—Block Six: Yoshida dampens both the print and the block, and then brushes a thin solution of black *sumi* ink on the block. He then registers the paper in the *kento*, places it, covered with newspaper, on the block, and rubs the *baren* over the newspaper-covered print. After the im-

pression is made, he again blots the print with newspaper.

Eighth Printing—Block Four: For this printing, Yoshida does not dampen the paper but uses it slightly drier. He brushes Talen's ultramarine blue on specific areas of the block. He uses the Talen's colors, which are more opaque and of greater brightness or intensity, to contrast with the more transparent watercolors. Because the paper was not damp when the impression was made, he does not need to blot the paper after the printing is done.

Ninth Printing—Block Three: Yoshida applies Talen's permanent purple to specific areas of the block, and prints from the block as he did in the eighth printing.

Tenth Printing—Block Five: Yoshida thinly brushes Holbein's sepia watercolor on only a part of the block, and then brushes water around the areas on which the paint has been brushed in order to soften and gradate the color at the edges of the form (135). He rubs the *baren* directly on the print,

136   137

which again has not been dampened, and therefore requires no blotting after he takes the impression.

Eleventh Printing—Block Six: Yoshida paints the central part of the form in block six with black *sumi* ink, and then prints the block twice.

Twelfth Printing—Block Seven: Yoshida applies Talen's permanent red violet directly from the tube to the block, and then brushes the color out on the block with a brush that he has dipped in water. He again uses the *baren* directly on the print. (He does not use several of the forms carved on the block at all in the printing, and later he cuts these forms away.)

Thirteenth Printing—Block Eight: Yoshida brushes black, Nicker poster paint quite thickly on the block (137) and prints the block as he did in the twelfth printing.

Fourteenth Printing—Block Seven: Yoshida brushes two colors, Talen's cobalt blue for the linear areas and vermilion for the round spot, on the block. Then he prints from the block (138).

Fifteenth Printing—Block Four: Yoshida brushes Talen's ultramarine blue on the round form and prints it quite opaquely.

Sixteenth Printing—Block One: To complete the print (color plate 36p), Yoshida mixes black *sumi* ink and Holbein's sepia watercolor, thins the mixture with water, and brushes the color on the block. With a rag, he lightly wipes some of the color from the central area of the form. He places the print, almost dry at this point, on the block and makes the impression. He uses the *baren* with a heavy pressure on the edges of the block and with a very light pressure on the center of the block. He does this to give a sharply defined edge.

138

139

112

Questions and Answers

Question: Do you have a theme or idea in mind before you start a print?

Hagiwara: Yes, I have a definite theme or idea before starting my work.

Kitaoka: I start a print only when the theme and idea have grown clear and definite in my mind. Printmaking, because of its very nature, requires that the whole process should be precisely worked out beforehand.

Kidokoro: The medium itself evokes in my mind a vague image, with which I begin my work. I feel that any theme that is literary, conventional or definite tends to weaken the plastic aspect of the picture; that is, the color, form, structure and so forth. Such themes also impose a restraint on creative activity, or lead to a type of repetition. I start thinking in direct contact with the medium without any preconception; that is, my thought reveals itself only through engagement with the medium. If "idea" is interpreted as "inspiration," then it can be said that I sometimes start my print that way.

Azechi: Yes, I start my work after deciding my theme and idea.

Yoshida: Sometimes I do. Although the final results may seem similar, I often use different processes, which can be classified into the following categories: When I start with a definite theme in mind, I make many small sketches in pencil or ink so that I may achieve the plastic representation of the theme, but I am not always successful because of the loss of the original ideas during the process. At other times, I start with a vague idea or emotion which I try to visualize from various angles or points of view. Occasionally I succeed in fixing it as a clear image, but the original idea often develops into another object. Many of my works are made through this latter process. Sometimes I start with no theme or idea and work directly with the material, particularly when using paper blocks. An action inspires me with an idea which decides or stimulates the next action. Forms and colors thus produced are gradually organized into a picture. Such attempts often end in utter failure; nevertheless, the results, when successful, please me primarily because of their spontaneity, which could not be attained by other methods. Sometimes, I find, quite by chance, in an automatic drawing, a part of a sketch, or stains on paper that which I have been looking for, and then I start to work it out into a definite image. In practice, however, the processes described above often merge or overlap. In my work the motive has little relation, if any, to the theme. The idea, in my view, has little to do with a work of art.

Question: What is it you generally wish to express in your work?

Hagiwara: Universal humanism.

Kitaoka: Decayed rafts, fishing villages, rocky seasides; Whatever subjects I choose, I want to express through them the profundity of nature and the feeling of eternity. This attitude may appear too seclusive or ignorant of our actual community, yet I believe in the end that it relates to a love of mankind.

Kidokoro: I want to catch and express in my work the image of the world—this world of tragedy. I want to portray the image of man as clearly as I conceive it in my mind.

Tajima: My motif is various. I start my work from a spiritual or a *sachlich* moment or metaphysical moment, so that what I want to express varies accordingly.

Azechi: The enigma of human emotion that one feels in the midst of nature.

Yoshida: It is hard to put into words. What I want to express is something that exists in the depth of humanity, unfrocked of all that is superficial, the simple humanity that I believe is common to all mankind. I want to make various phases of human vitality visible by plastic representation. This answer seems somewhat too easy and makes me hesitant to assert it as a satisfactory one. After all, it is something that I cannot verbally express, for, if I could, I wouldn't have to make pictures.

Question: What do you want your work to communicate to the viewer?

Hagiwara: Something that can purify the viewer's mind.

Kitaoka: What I have stated before, a feeling of eternity. At the same time, I am interested in the viewer's response to my technique.

Kidokoro: If my work could be, for the viewer who has no prejudices, an object that is beautiful and full of energy, I could ask for nothing better.

Tajima: I leave my works totally to the viewer's interpretation.

Azechi: I want to express my thoughts on the social responsibilities of all human beings. I hope to express this idea through the representation of the grandeur of nature, though this is a difficult task with my limited ability.

Yoshida: I don't care what it may communicate, even if it be something quite different from what I have in mind. I would be satisfied if it could move the viewer, be his reaction sympathetic or hostile.

Question: What aspects of the *ukiyo-e* tradition do you feel have value for you?

Hagiwara: The point that it is closely related with the life of the common people.

Kitaoka: It is true that we have adopted the tools and materials of *ukiyo-e*, as they have been handed down to us in their finished state. As for the technique or expression, we owe practically nothing to the *ukiyo-e* artists, since modern printmaking started as a negation of this tradition. The techniques used by the *ukiyo-e* artists are still worthy of study though, for one might yet find methods that can be utilized in the making of modern prints.

Kidokoro: For me, the only significance the *ukiyo-e* has is that the medium is the wood block. Its subject matter is apart from my interest.

Tajima: My question is how to deny the *ukiyo-e* tradition.

Azechi: That part of the *ukiyo-e* tradition that reflects the feeling of the common people.

Yoshida: Only the tradition of its tools and materials has value for me. When considered as a pictorial art, *ukiyo-e* has nothing in common with our work. Nevertheless, if we should take it in a more abstracted sense of the word, such as racial trait in regard to sensibility or feeling, it can be said that *ukiyo-e*, as well as other classical arts of Japan, has definite significance.

Question: Does any aspect of politics or religion enter into your art?

Hagiwara: I don't consciously try to express anything political or religious in my work, but in a wide sense these factors cannot be avoided.

Kitaoka: My works are not related in any way to politics or religion. Yet, as I stated before, I stand in awe of nature and often feel an impulse to plunge into it. This feeling, in the sense that it seeks harmony between man and nature, might be called religious.

Kidokoro: My wishes for what actual politics should be may be reflected in my work, though not in any apparent form. As for religion, I have never intended to express it in my work. The truth of art, in my opinion, lies somewhere else.

Tajima: I don't feel that politics or religion enters my works, but the *way* of politics or religion of this country has something to do with my way of thinking.

Azechi: In the depths of my creativity, my thoughts of politics and religion are included.

Yoshida: I don't think any aspect of politics or religion enters into my art. I am interested, however, in primitive religions and magic cults, as I feel they manifest the vitality of a less complicated humanity, which modern people have lost. I have based quite a few works on these motives, although, in the strict sense of the word, they cannot be called religious.

Question: Because artists are much more international, know what is being done everywhere in the world and have access to reproductions and original works of art, it is often difficult if not impossible, to relate a work of contemporary art to the nationality of the artist. In the light of this statement, do you feel you are expressing something that has a particular Japanese significance—aside from the fact that you are Japanese working in Japan—or are you more concerned with a universal or international point of view or style?

Hagiwara: Today it is necessary to look at and express things from the universal point of view. Yet I want to express something Japanese through that style of expression.

Kitaoka: I once believed in the international style or in that way of thinking because I felt more or less obliged to do so. At present, though, I feel that I should express something Japanese, or more precisely something representing myself—who happens to be Japanese. This, however, does not mean selecting such subjects as Japanese gardens or Buddhist icons —the accomplishments of Japanese art of the past—for this appeals only to foreigners in their search for the *exotica* of the Orient. I feel that I should derive my creative activity from the deeper thoughts of the Orient, from a feeling that has its roots in Japanese nature and the Japanese way of living.

Kidokoro: Despite the comment [aside from the fact you are Japanese], I can't help observing, above all, that I am a Japanese working in Japan. Therefore, I don't want to make the same mistakes as they did in pursuing Chinese style in France or the Oriental mood in Holly-wood, which are fundamentally based on their misunderstanding of those traditions. Japan is changing as well as the rest of the world. The traditions in Japan are preserved, though unsatisfactorily, by private museums and the government. Even with this protection, some of the traditions and the spirit inherent in them have lost their appeal. In my estimation, true tradition must have the force to revive even after destruction. Let's let those that perish remain so. Isn't that a beautiful attitude also? Nothing is more pleasing to me than to live in the world of Manyō, Genji Monogatari or Saikaku, or to feel the world of Sōtatsu, Korin, Hokusai and Sharaku become as fresh and lively as ever in our world. These inheritances give me a feeling for life. It is futile, though, to follow indiscriminately external forms of tradi-tional art. We should rather strive to follow in the direction in which the tradition has pointed. The world is growing more homogeneous, and as a reaction to this development one could be inclined to stick with the old traditions simply because they seem less uncertain. But this attitude is merely self-deception, and in the creative arts leads nowhere but to local folk crafts. It is the task of the artist to resist the encroachment of conformism in our world by using the force of his reason to search for universal validity.

Tajima: I don't particularly try to express a Japanese theme. What interests me is how I encounter and solve the problems that surround me, regardless of their being Japanese or universal.

Azechi: I want to conceive my life and thought from a universal and international point of view, and upon this basis I wish my work to be Japanese.

Yoshida: Lately, I have not consciously pursued anything particularly Japanese in motif or process, but I don't intend to be more international either. Whether the results of my work are Japanese or international is a matter for the viewer to decide. I consider Japan very important in my mind, but to emphasize it in my work by attempting to adopt a "Japanese" style of expression is something quite outside of my interest—in fact, it is almost repulsive. Frankly, I am inclined to think very critically of such trends, especially as it applies to the Japanese wood-block print. Indeed, it is surprising that so many works have been made that aim at such a superficial Japanese mood! I admit that the conscious pursuit of Japanese themes is meaningful, but I believe that in this subject area there are far more important and more profound aspects to be treated. So-called *shibui* tone, a somewhat moist texture, a particular structure of spatial elements, simplicity, or Zen that is superficially understood—why should we confine "Japanese" to these aspects only? Such a view is quite narrow and should be rejected not only by Japanese artists but also by foreign art-lovers. In my opinion, Japan has many other and quite different features that should be emphasized. There are quite a few people who find my works "Japanese" also, but mainly for those elements other than what is normally thought of as "Japanese." For example, they associate my work with *Otsu-e,* or see a likeness between my color and that of multicolored folk crafts, or point out that my form is akin to the dolls of the "Boy's Festival," or to *Jomon doki,* the archaic earthenwares, although I was not conscious of these identities before. It is true that I like these things and that I passed through a period during which I consciously intended to express something

116

"Japanese" with obviously Japanese motif, such as Buddhist icons and Japanese gardens. This was during 1953 and 1954. My visit to Mexico in 1955 was instrumental in changing my way of thinking. For the first time I was able to emancipate myself from the "Japanese" orientation and express something that was my own. In practice it was first done with form and then with color. Now I don't care what terms are used to describe my work, whether Japanese, Mexican or cosmopolitan—though, of course, I shall be pleased if they call it Japanese in the true sense of the word. If perchance it earns a reputation as "primitive," this will surely be a cause for smiling. Anyway, I think it is quite unimportant how or under which terms the external style of a work of art is named.

Question: What are your thoughts concerning content—that is, the idea, story, theme and message, and form—plastic values, design, structure, spatial relationships and so forth? Content and form cannot be completely separated, of course; but which of the areas do you value most? How do you consciously relate the areas of content and form.

Hagiwara: Since spatial relationship involves everything else in the question, I consider it most important.

Kitaoka: Form is meaningless without content, so I consider content more important. However, it is true that content itself cannot make a work of art unless it has an appropriate form. Form may take precedence over content in the immature stage of a work of art, but in a consummate work, form and content are absolutely inseparable and should blend together in a perfect unity. Though I have a clear vision of content, I always have to suffer in search of the proper technical solution for its ideal form, encompassing the plastic values, design, structure and spatial relationships.

Kidokoro: I give priority to plastic elements; that is, design, color and structure rather than the content or idea or story or theme. But both areas are inseparable and practically one thing for the artist.

Tajima: Of style and content, I consider the former more important. Of course, style and content cannot be clearly separated—sometimes a style itself makes its content, whereas there are cases when the content decides its style. Yet the work of plastic art is fundamentally an art that is expressed through an object. In my case, how to weave the content into my work in considered again and again at every stage of the process.

Azechi: (no answer)

Yoshida: I consider content more important, though I am skeptical about even attempting to divide a work of art into the two categories. It is of course impossible to deal with any work consciously in the two aspects. For me, it is more acceptable to conceive content as plasticity and form as technique—form is the means to realize content, and content will naturally make its own form, or content is a body, and form is only its clothing—various ideas occur in my mind, but they are far from sufficient to explain the heart of the matter. If the Japanese *hanga* (prints) can be divided into *han* (block) and *ga* (picture), I would not hesitate to give priority to *ga*; in this case, *ga* is content and *han* is the means for form.

Glossary

ategawa : The laminated paper disc in which the *baren*, a coil of bamboo cord, is contained.

baren : Specifically, a flat coil of twisted bamboo fibers. Generally, a circular pad consisting of an *ategawa*, *baren* and *barengawa*, constructed of paper and bamboo materials, used for rubbing the reverse side of the print placed upon the wood-block surface in order to make an impression.

barengawa : The single bamboo husk or sheath used to cover the printing surface of the *baren*. The ends are folded over and twisted to form a grip across the back of the *baren*.

bokuju : A black carbon ink in liquid form.

camellia oil : A lubricant obtained from the seeds of a genus of evergreen tree or shrub (*C. Sasaqua*) found in Japan and China. The oil is is used to lubricate and preserve the printing surface of the *baren*.

Daruma : A Buddhist saint who, in Japan, is popularly depicted as being limbless.

dosa : A sizing made from a high quality animal glue and alum thinned with water and applied to paper to give it a controllable absorbency.

-e : A Japanese suffix that means picture.

Edo : The former eastern capital of Japan, now called Tokyo.

ga : A Japanese word meaning picture or drawing.

gampi : A shrublike plant (*Wickstroemia shikokiana*) found in Japan, whose inner bark yields a fiber for making the *wa-shi* papers.

glaze : A coat of semitransparent color applied over a painted surface.

han : A wood block for printing. Also the seal or personal stamp of the Japanese used to imprint an individual's name or "*han*."

hanga : The term generally used to describe the modern Japanese prints.

hanga torinoko : See *torinoko*.

hosho : *Wa-shi* papers made from the fibers of the *kozo*.

hosho-shi : *Wa-shi* papers made from the fibers of the *kozo* combined with paper pulp.

intaglio : An etching technique that is also used in wood block when printing from carved out lines or forms in the wood block which retain the printing ink or color medium.

kento : The registry guides carved into the wood block itself to indicate the correct, precise placement of each sheet of print paper.

key block : The block traditionally made to serve as a guide for designing and registering the subsequent color blocks.

kizuki-hosho : A *wa-shi* paper made of pure *kozo*.

kozo : A small tree (*Brousenntia kaji-*

noki) found in Japan, whose inner bark yields a fiber for making *wa-shi* papers.

kozo-shi : A general term given to *wa-shi* papers that are formed from the *kozo* pulp.

mica : A semitransparent mineral powder or ground inner surface of sea shells used to add a surface richness and glitter to the print.

mitsumata : A small tree (*Edgeworthia papyrifera*) found in Japan, whose inner bark yields a fiber for making *wa-shi* papers.

nikawa : A high-grade animal glue, similar to rabbit glue, used for sizing and as a binder for pigments.

nishiki-e : The polychrome prints from Harunobu onward, also called "Brocade Pictures."

nishino-uchi : A *wa-shi* paper made basically of *kozo* pulp but also with the addition of wood pulp.

nori : A paste made from rice flour.

otsu-e : Popular, Buddhistic hand-painted sheets of the seventeenth century. So called from the village of Otsu, near Kyoto, where they were originally made and sold.

rawan : Called lauan, it is one of the Philippine mahoganies; medium textured and straight grained, a medium-weight hardwood; easy to carve.

registry : The accurate placement of each sheet of paper upon each block used in the printing sequence in order to make a controlled print.

relief : The projection of forms and lines from a flat surface so that they stand above the surrounding surface that, in woodcuts for example, has been carved away.

rice paper : A general term that is used by non-Japanese to describe Japanese papers. The term is neither accurate nor usable and is a mistranslation from the Japanese word, *gampi*.

rodo oil : Translated rote oil, it is a sulfonated castor oil used as a neutral detergent when mixed with a large quantity of water. It is also used as a surface activating agent.

samurai : The class of military retainers of the *daimio* or feudal lords during the former feudal system in Japan.

-*shi* : A Japanese suffix that means paper.

shina : A fine textured, straight-grained bass wood (Japanese linden) that is light, soft and easily worked.

shoji : A Japanese sliding door or window that is constructed of a wooden frame covered with a white translucent paper.

size : A solution of glue, alum and water. See *dosa*.

sumi : A black carbon ink that is made into a hard cake form.

toishi : A stone used for sharpening tools.

torinoko : A *wa-shi* paper made basically from *mitsumata* and *gampi*.

There are many grades and types of *torinoko* that use various combinations of *mitsumata*, *gampi* and wood pulp, such as *hanga torinoko*, which was developed specifically for printmaking.

tororo-aoi : A plant root (*Hibiscus Manihot*) that yields a mucilaginous material used in making *wa-shi* papers.

ukiyo-e : "Floating world" paintings and prints of the *Edo* period.

waka : A distinctively Japanese poetic form.

wa-shi : Papers made by the traditional Japanese hand methods.

wood pulp : The fibers derived from coniferous trees and used in papermaking.

yo-shi : The Japanese term for papers made by mechanical methods and machinery.

Sources of Materials and Supplies

Tokyo's Yoseido Gallery, a leading exhibitor of contemporary Japanese prints, can supply the reader with those art supplies produced in Japan. All materials used for wood-block printing, including those described in this book (paper, tools, paints, dyes, etc.), may be obtained by addressing your inquiries to: The Yoseido Gallery, Art Supply Section, No. 5, 5-chome, Nishi Ginza, Chuo-ku, Tokyo, Japan.

Sources of Additional Information

General:

About Prints, Stanley W. Hayter. London, 1962.
Printmaking, by Gabor Peterdi. New York, 1959.
Printmaking Today, by Jules Heller. New York, 1958.

Woodblock:

Japanese Woodblock Prints, by Umetaro Azechi. Tokyo, 1963.
Woodcuts, by John R. Biggs. London, 1958.
The Relief Print, edited by E. W. Watson and Norman Kent. New York, 1945.
Color Woodcut, by John Platt. New York, 1938.

Design, Color, Drawing:

Vision in Motion, by L. Moholy-Nagy. Chicago, 1947.
Language of Vision, by Gyorgy Kepes. Chicago, 1944.
The Natural Way Draw, by Kimon Nicolaides. Boston, 1941.

Critical and Historical Works:

Masters of the Japanese Print, by Richard Lane. London, 1962.
The Japanese Print, by J. Hillier. London, 1960.
Modern Japanese Prints, by Oliver Statler. Tokyo, 1956.
The Floating World, by James A. Michener. New York, 1954.
A Book of Fine Prints, by Carl Zigrosser. New York, 1948.